D0075655

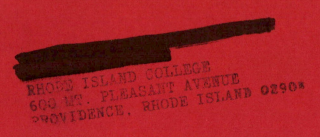

# Teaching Through Modality Strengths: Concepts and Practices

Walter B. Barbe
Raymond H. Swassing

with Michael N. Milone, Jr.

**Zaner-Bloser, Inc.**
Columbus, Ohio

ISBN No. 0–88309–100–3
Library of Congress Catalog No. 79–66953
Reorder No. 840030–0

# Contents

**Preface** . . . . . . . . . . . . . . . . . . . . . . . . . . . . . . . . . . . . . . . vii

CHAPTER I
**The Concept of Modality** . . . . . . . . . . . . . . . . . . . . . . . . . .1
    Definition . . . . . . . . . . . . . . . . . . . . . . . . . . . . . . . . . . . .1
    Three Views of Modality . . . . . . . . . . . . . . . . . . . . . . . . .3
    The Educationally Relevant Modalities . . . . . . . . . . . . . . .5
    Dominant, Secondary, and Mixed Modalities . . . . . . . . . . .6
    Why Teach through Modality Strengths? . . . . . . . . . . . . . .7
    Fundamentals of Modality-Based Instruction . . . . . . . . . . .13
    Conclusion . . . . . . . . . . . . . . . . . . . . . . . . . . . . . . . . . . .16

CHAPTER II
**The History of Modality-Based Instruction** . . . . . . . . . .18
    Commentary . . . . . . . . . . . . . . . . . . . . . . . . . . . . . . . . . .28

CHAPTER III
**Identifying Modality Strengths** . . . . . . . . . . . . . . . . . . . .31
    Introduction . . . . . . . . . . . . . . . . . . . . . . . . . . . . . . . . . . .31
    Previous Efforts at Assessing Modality Strengths . . . . . . . .32
    Development of the Swassing-Barbe Modality Index . . . . . .34
    Description of the SBMI . . . . . . . . . . . . . . . . . . . . . . . . . .35
    Administration of the SBMI . . . . . . . . . . . . . . . . . . . . . . .36
    Scoring the SBMI . . . . . . . . . . . . . . . . . . . . . . . . . . . . . .39
    Interpretation of Modality Percentage Scores . . . . . . . . . . .40
    Observable Characteristics Indicative
       of Modality Strength . . . . . . . . . . . . . . . . . . . . . . . . . .43
    Summary . . . . . . . . . . . . . . . . . . . . . . . . . . . . . . . . . . . .46

**CHAPTER IV**

**Standardization of the SBMI** . . . . . . . . . . . . . . . . . .47
    Psychometric Properties of the SBMI . . . . . . . . . . . . . .48
    The Relationship between Modality Strengths
        and Sex, Handedness, and Grade . . . . . . . . . . . . . . . . .51
    Summary . . . . . . . . . . . . . . . . . . . . . . . . . . . . . . . . .54

**CHAPTER V**

**The Practice of Modality-Based Instruction** . . . . . . . . .55
    What Is Modality-Based Instruction? . . . . . . . . . . . . . . .55
    Initial Teaching Strategies . . . . . . . . . . . . . . . . . . . . . .58
    The Point of Intervention . . . . . . . . . . . . . . . . . . . . . .62
    Modality-Based Instruction in Basic Skill Areas . . . . . . . . .64
    Modality-Based Instruction in Reading . . . . . . . . . . . . . .65
    Modality-Based Instruction in Handwriting . . . . . . . . . . . .66
    Modality-Based Instruction in Arithmetic . . . . . . . . . . . . .67
    Modality-Based Instruction in Spelling . . . . . . . . . . . . . .68
    Summary . . . . . . . . . . . . . . . . . . . . . . . . . . . . . . . . .70

**CHAPTER VI**

**Summary** . . . . . . . . . . . . . . . . . . . . . . . . . . . . . . . . .71
    The Definition of Modality . . . . . . . . . . . . . . . . . . . . .71
    Modality Strengths . . . . . . . . . . . . . . . . . . . . . . . . . .71
    Measuring Modality Strengths . . . . . . . . . . . . . . . . . . .71
    Modality-Based Instruction . . . . . . . . . . . . . . . . . . . . .72
    The History of Modality-Based Instruction . . . . . . . . . . . .73
    The Promise of Modality-Based Instruction . . . . . . . . . . . .73

**Appendix A** . . . . . . . . . . . . . . . . . . . . . . . . . . . . . . .78

**Appendix B** . . . . . . . . . . . . . . . . . . . . . . . . . . . . . . .85

**Selected Readings** . . . . . . . . . . . . . . . . . . . . . . . . .101

**Index of Names** . . . . . . . . . . . . . . . . . . . . . . . . . .109

**Index of Subjects** . . . . . . . . . . . . . . . . . . . . . . . . .110

# Preface

Dr. Paul Witty, one of America's foremost psychologists and educators, once related a story about an experience he had with an elementary school child. After working with the child for several hours, the child had still failed to learn a certain task. In frustration, Dr. Witty pushed the materials away and said to the child, "What's wrong with you?" Without a moment's hesitation, the child replied, "What's wrong with me? What's wrong with you? *You* what's wrong!"

This story describes a feeling that each of us has had. We try everything and the child still cannot learn. What's wrong with the child? We know that the child is not at fault. We have not found the key as to how this child learns.

The purpose of this book is to help teachers find that key. To our way of thinking, the key lies within the child—the child's modality strength. The approach described in this book provides the teacher with a means of identifying the child's modality strength, and then recommends strategies that capitalize upon that particular learning strength. In no way are the goals of education changed; we simply outline more efficient ways to achieve these goals.

The methods upon which this book focuses are strength oriented. We know our own weak areas, learned no doubt through years of trial, error, and frustration. As adults, we studiously avoid these areas, and direct our activities instead to our areas of strength. Children, however, are denied this luxury. The traditional pattern for the child in an academic setting has been to be confronted with failure, and then to be given seemingly endless hours of practice, not in the areas of strength, but in weaknesses. Must the goal of education be to find out what a child cannot do and then to emphasize these deficits? Is there not a way that a child can use his or her strengths to overcome deficiencies, and enjoy doing it?

We believe that there is a way to teach that is both enjoyable and helps children overcome their deficiencies. The method, described in this text, focuses more on how the child learns than what is actually learned. Our philosophy is that once there is a clear understanding of how the child learns, then almost any relevant topic can be learned.

Because we are process rather than content oriented, it is possible to misinterpret our meaning and infer that we are minimizing the importance of basic skills. Quite the opposite is true. Basic skills are important, for without them, there is little hope that a child will become an independent learner. We do feel, however, that the goal of education must not become only the acquisition, in isolation, of a predetermined set of minimal skills. Such a goal limits the potential of every student, and denies to many students the richness that makes life worthwhile. The goal of education must be to help every child achieve to the limit of his or her ability. Through the methods outlined in this text, this goal can become a reality.

Appreciation is expressed to the teachers and children throughout the country who participated in field testing, demonstrations, workshops, and research projects. Not all could possibly be named, but particular appreciation must be expressed to Ms. Lois Braun and Ms. Sue Lyons of the Santa Monica Unified School District (Santa Monica, California), Dr. Virginia Lucas of Wittenberg University (Springfield, Ohio), Mr. James Wilhide of the South Carolina Department of Education (Columbia, South Carolina), Dr. Harry Hurst and Dr. Stephen MacIntosh of the Indian River County School Board (Vero Beach, Florida), and Mr. J. Owen Long of the Rockingham County Public Schools (Harrisonburg, Virginia). And to Molly Rodgers, Judith Harlan, Marjory Kline, Kenneth Kreitner for their editorial work at various stages, and to Constance Gross and Helen Spencer for typing, the authors give their thanks.

# CHAPTER I

# The Concept of Modality

This chapter is an introduction to the concepts that serve as the foundations for this text. A definition of modality is presented, this construct is related to other psychological processes, and the fundamentals of teaching to modality strengths are discussed.

## Definition

A modality is any of the sensory channels through which an individual receives and retains information. A critical component of this definition is the phrase "receives and retains," since it implies that sensation, perception, and memory constitute what we are calling modality. Because these three processes are the essence of learning itself, the modalities can be called the keys to learning.

In order to give the reader a clear understanding of the concept of modality we are proposing, it is important to comment upon its constituent elements—sensation, perception, and memory. A sensation occurs when an object or energy source from the environment impinges upon an individual. The flare of a match in a darkened room and the sudden cry of a night animal generate sensations. The most important characteristic of a sensation is that little or no meaning is attached to the stimulation. In the first example cited above, the match would be sensed as a "light" by a naive observer. In other words, there would be no reason to suspect that the "light" was caused by a match rather than by a flashlight or some other luminescent object. A sensation is the purest interaction between an individual and the environment.

When some meaning is ascribed to a sensation, we step into the realm of perceptions. Epstein provides a definition of perception that is clearly distinguishable from that of sensation: "Perception is an . . . inferred process that intervenes between the measurable stimulus conditions and the measurable overt response" (1967, p. 10). In Epstein's definition, sensation would correspond to the reception of the stimulus condition. Once this occurs, the individual can call upon his or her past experiences to relate the sensation to a previously occurring event. In other words, the individual attaches meaning to the sensation, and behaves accordingly. The behavior in question might be overt, such as lighting a fire with the match of the example described above, or it may be covert. Reading is an example of a covert behavior. The printed words serve as the stimuli. The reader senses the images on the page, relates them to real or imagined events, and generates images that are consistent with the intentions of the writer.

Implicit in the definition of perception is the existence of what we call memory. How else could meaning be ascribed to a sensation, other than to recall information from a storehouse of some kind? This storehouse is memory.

Psychologists are almost universal in their agreement that memory consists of at least two components, one of which deals with information on a short term basis, while the other retains information for a longer period of time. An easily understandable analogy for explaining long and short term memory has been described by Klatzky (1975). A carpenter's workshop is likely to have at least one table and several shelves upon which to store tools and materials. The table can be compared to short term memory. On it, a small number of items for immediate use can be stored. If the items are not used at once, and additional items are placed on the table, then something must give and several of the items will fall from the table. Much the same can be said about short term memory. Items, such as a telephone number retrieved from the directory, must be used at once. If not, they will be lost as other numbers are needed. It is comparatively easy to remember one telephone number at a time. When we attempt to go to the directory and memorize more than one number at a time, the task becomes more difficult.

The carpenter's shelves, on the other hand, can be used to store the items that are not of immediate use. By shifting tools or materials from the table to the shelves, additional workspace on the table can be provided, and the items on the table can be spared possible damage by dropping them. Thus, long term memory serves as a receptacle for those images that need to be preserved in an undamaged state, and as a storehouse for some of the items that are cluttering up the short term memory.

Sensation, perception, and memory are obviously closely related phenomena. Sensation underlies both memory and perception, for without the reception of the stimulus from the environment, neither perception nor memory could function. The senses provide the raw material for perception and memory. Perception, on the other hand, is the only means by which sensations can be organized in a useful manner. Useless sensations can be ignored, while those sensations which have immediate or long-range bearing on the functioning of the individual can be retained. And of course, they are retained in the memory, for brief periods of time in the short term memory, and for much longer periods of time in the long term memory.

## Three Views of Modality

The definition of modality to which we subscribe is a broad one that comprises sensation, perception, and memory. There are other approaches to understanding modality, however, of which the reader should be aware. Summarized below are two of these differing views of modality, as well as a reiteration of our own perspective for the purpose of comparison.

*Modality as a fixed neurological characteristic.* As the title implies, this view treats modality as a physiological characteristic with which an individual is endowed. Modality strength is determined chiefly by hereditary factors, and it undergoes little change between childhood and adulthood. This view is typified by Wepman's comment that "children who strongly prefer the auditory pathway appear never to lose their preference but remain auditory learners all of their lives" (1971, p. 56).

When modality is defined as a fixed neurological characteristic, it is equated with sensation only. That is, modality is localized in the pathway between the sensory organ and the brain region where the sensation is processed. Differences in modality strengths between individuals can be attributed to differences in the efficiency of the sensory pathways, and the environment appears to have little or no influence on modality strengths.

The most obvious characteristic of this perspective is its simplicity. Modality strengths are readily explained and simply researched. The chief disadvantage of the approach is that it ignores the foremost modifier of human behavior, the environment. Any perspective that fails to acknowledge the central role of learning in human development is not acceptable to most educators and psychologists.

Although we do not feel that modality strength can be fully explained by approaching it as a fixed neurological characteristic, we do agree that each one of us is predisposed to certain modality strengths. Neonates differ within themselves and from other neonates with respect to many features, and it is reasonable to assume that modality strengths may be among these features.

*Modality as a preference.* If adults were asked how they learn best—by seeing, hearing, or doing—many of them would be able to give a definite answer. This is the basis for describing modality as a preference. It reflects an individual's personal opinion concerning the modality through which he or she learns best.

Treating modality as a preference has one great appeal: the source of information is the individual. Thus, the preference is valid in that it is based upon extensive personal experience. On the other hand, personal preference is not very reliable, since most individuals are not well trained observers of their own behavior. Their judgments will be inconsistent, and will reflect the immediate situation rather than long standing behaviors.

Few adults and almost no children have a clear picture of the conditions under which they learn best. When pressed for an answer, most people respond in a socially acceptable manner, or describe a situation in which exemplary learning took place.

The former response is typical of a teenager who says that he or she has an auditory preference. This might not be how the adolescent actually prefers to learn, but it is how the respondent thinks his or her peers prefer to learn.

When individuals describe an exemplary learning experience, they assume that because rapid learning took place, the modality characteristics of the situation reflect their modality preferences. This might be the case, but more often than not, the reinforcement or motivational aspects of the situation are responsible for the rapid learning. Take the instance of the child who is subjected to the "sink or swim" approach to swimming. By throwing the child into the pool and shouting directions, the instructor is using an auditory approach. The child who learns to swim in this way may conclude that audition is his or her preferred modality. A more astute observer will note that the mode of instruction had less to do with the rapid learning than the consequences associated with not learning to swim.

With individuals who are sufficiently perceptive to observe their own behaviors objectively, the preference approach is useful. But since few persons fall into this category, this approach is not generally appropriate.

*Modality as a measurable behavior.* The concept of modality that is presented in this text aims at being comprehensive and functional. It considers all the links of the chain between a sensation and the individual's resultant behavior, and defines modality strength operationally as the ability of an individual to perform an academically relevant task in each of the major modalities. As such, the definition we are proposing acknowledges the role of both heredity and the environment in shaping an individual's modality strengths.

We also acknowledge that modality preferences exist. A qualification to this acknowledgement is that the manner in which an individual is most comfortable receiving information is not always consonant with the way in which information is most efficiently received and processed. Throughout the text, then, modality strength will be equated with functioning in each modality and not modality preference.

## The Educationally Relevant Modalities

As was mentioned previously, the modalities are the channels through which people receive and retain information. Organizing instruction around one or more of these channels is called modality-based instruction. The three modalities that have the greatest utility in the classroom are the visual, auditory, and kinesthetic.

There is no need to define the terms *auditory* and *visual,* since there is little disagreement concerning the meanings of these words. The meaning of the term *kinesthetic,* however, varies from source to source, and therefore merits clarification.

When we refer to the kinesthetic modality, we are including large muscle movements, small muscle movements, and the sense of touch. This definition is more extensive than that to which some other authors and researchers subscribe. It is possible to separate these three abilities and treat them individually, and in some instances, it may be beneficial to do so. For practical purposes, however, discussing large muscle, small muscle, and tactile abilities under one heading reflects the behavior of children better than does treating each component separately. In the classroom, there are very few occasions when only the tactile sense is used; the same holds true for large and small muscle movements. Certainly, the relative mix of these components varies from child to child, but in almost all children, the three components are present.

The assessment method described in this text measures kinesthesia as a composite ability. The majority of the proponents of modality-based education agree with the definition we propose, and the curriculum recommendations we make in later chapters hinge upon treating the kinesthetic modality as a combination of large muscle, small muscle, and tactile abilities.

## Dominant, Secondary, and Mixed Modalities

An individual's dominant modality is that channel through which information is processed most efficiently. In elementary school age children, dominant modalities are often readily observed. Through maturation, children's modalities become integrated as they discover cognitive strategies to transfer information from one modality to another. As a result, it is generally more difficult to identify a single dominant modality of an adult. When a situation is stressful, or when the consequences associated with an event are great, an adult will resort to his or her dominant modality. In everyday situations, however, adults are usually able to process information in whatever mode it is presented.

Besides a dominant modality, many people evidence a secondary modality upon which they can rely when the situation demands it. Secondary modalities are important in the educational process because it is not always possible to capitalize upon a child's dominant modality. When this is the case, the teacher can direct the learning activity to the child's secondary modality.

By definition, a secondary modality is not so efficient as its dominant counterpart. A secondary modality does, however, complement a dominant modality; that is, instead of interfering with the functioning of the dominant modality, a secondary modality enhances it. Children with a dominant kinesthetic modality and a secondary visual modality are not at a disadvantage when a lesson is presented in either of these modes. If the child needs additional explanation or practice on a skill after it has been presented in his or her dominant mode, the teacher can utilize techniques which allow the child to revert to the secondary mode for support.

Mixed modalities occur when no single modality is clearly dominant. Since the proportion of persons with mixed modalities is larger among adults than children, we suspect that cognitive maturity and the opportunity to practice in all three modalities are the principal reasons that mixed modalities occur. For the most part, children with mixed modality strengths have an easier time in the classroom since they are able to process information in two or three modalities with equal efficiency.

## Why Teach Through Modality Strengths?

The question "Why teach through modality strengths?" can be answered first by realizing that the greatest concern of teachers is assisting their students to reach their full potential. Basing instruction upon modality strengths is a way of accomplishing this goal. Further, we feel that: modality-based instruction is logical; modality-based instruction is already practiced by teachers to some extent; and research supports the contention that modality-based instruction works.

*Modality-based instruction is logical.* At some time, every teacher faces the situation in which she or he is asked to do something that seems illogical. Whether or not the end justified the means is not the question; the most important consideration is that when we are asked to do something illogical, we do so only reluctantly. With respect to modality-based educational practices, however, the approach is logical. The following examples illustrate this point.

Have you ever known a child who asked to "see" something? Yet when the child got the chance to "see" the object or item, he or she immediately picked it up, juggled the object as if mentally weighing it, tapped it on the desk, possibly smelled it, and manipulated the object physically for some time. How about the youngster who learned very quickly from flash cards but did not like the "listening corner" with the tape recorder and headsets? Have you ever worked with a child who could not seem to remember a verbal message to deliver to the principal, but if the child wrote out the message he or she could recall that same message for two or three days?

If you have ever known children such as these, then you probably know why teaching through modality strengths makes sense. Because people are unique, they learn differently. Teaching through modality strengths capitalizes on these individual differences to increase the rate of learning by providing information through the most efficient channel for each child. If a certain child learns most efficiently by listening, is it not common sense to provide many auditory activities for that child? By way of contrast, does it make sense to try to teach that child number facts by flashcards rather than using tape recorded examples?

Some people gain information best through visual experiences, others through auditory experiences, and others through kinesthetic activities. To know which approach is the best for any given child is the first step; to plan activities that utilize these strengths is the second.

***Modality-based instruction is already practiced by teachers to some extent.*** When the initial efforts were being undertaken to introduce behavior modification into the classroom, one of the rationales supporting the use of this new practice was that "teachers are doing it already, and it is helpful if they know what they are doing." A similar argument holds for modality-based instruction: you probably do it already, so it is advantageous to know what you are doing.

Described below are visits to three classrooms. Each of the classrooms represents emphasis on a different modality. The major emphasis of Room 113 is auditory; as such, the classroom, the instruction, and the activities can be characterized as strongly auditory. Classroom 114 accentuates the kinesthetic modality, while Classroom 115 is markedly visual.

*Room 113, The Auditory Classroom:* The physical organization of this classroom is not immediately noticeable. Teacher and student desks are grouped together toward the front and center of the room. The reading table and chairs are behind and to the left of the center of the room. The open shelves are neat but organized in no particular fashion. The chalkboard is at the opposite end of the room from the teacher's desk. The chalkboard contains the morning "news report" and some tic-tac-toe games played by the children. There is one bulletin board in the room with a seasonal display on it. Two learning centers and a listening station are along the right side of the classroom.

The listening station has a tape recorder and a record player. There are numerous tapes and records that provide instruction in basic skills, plus some records of sounds and music. Each of the learning centers has a cassette recorder in plain sight. The directions for each center are on cassette tapes.

Instruction in this classroom is mainly in the form of verbal discussion and lecture. Student talk is encouraged, and language lessons are accompanied by much discussion. Reading aloud is stressed. Reading instruction is built on phonics lessons. There are frequent "spelling bees." The children are encouraged to do verbal math problems and games, and respond orally to flashcards.

Student small group interaction is encouraged. Small groups are organized for skill instruction, games, and for enrichment activities.

There is a constant "buzz" of activity as students chat back and forth about their lessons and other activities.

*Room 114, The Kinesthetic Classroom:* The physical organization in this classroom is not evident at all. The teacher's desk is out of the way in the far left corner. Items on the desk are in disarray; the desk is used mainly as readily accessible storage space for blocks, beads, jar lids, scissors, and other assorted items. The student desks are lined up along the left wall with wide aisles between rows. The center of the room is open space. Beyond the open space is the chalkboard. The chalkboard gives evidence of much use. The open shelf-space contains many items such as blocks, counters, models, diagrams, and construction materials. The shelves are organized by activities: art supplies, books, models, student-made materials. Around the room are many examples of student-made art pieces, including macrame, string art, and car and airplane models. The bulletin board is near the teacher's desk and contains geometric drawings by the children. There are no particular learning centers.

The learning aids in this classroom are of the three-dimensional, manipulative type. Cones, cubes, pyramids, rulers, protractors, clay, crayons, sandpaper, both wood and plastic blocks are numerous. An antique fortress is under construction on the table in one corner; a model of the DNA molecule is on top of a shelf; a mannequin rests on a stand near other science materials.

Much instruction takes place in the open space in the center of the room. Acting out a scene or activities occurs frequently. The teacher provides guidance for fine motor tasks. Instructional examples are accompanied by models and gestures. The children are encouraged to write spelling words, either at their desks or on the chalkboard. Unknown words are traced. Each child has crayons that are used frequently.

The children move freely about the room from one task to another. They go to the chalkboard to work out a math problem or get some objects to help calculate. Group activities involve acting out a scene or situation as well as discussion. Talking is tolerated as long as it does not interfere with others.

*Room 115, The Visual Classroom:* The physical organization in this classroom is immediately clear. The student desks are organized neatly in groups facing the teacher's desk. On the desk is a daily schedule for the class for small groups. There are several bulletin boards about the room, each colorfully decorated and displaying material relating to some element of the current lessons. There are three learning centers identified by attention-getting artwork. The math center contains numerous graphs and pictures of math examples. The materials are neatly organized about the room. The teacher's desk is the center of small group and individual conferences. It is neat and contains no distracting papers or objects. Numerous posters, signs, and pictures are displayed about the room. The letters of the alphabet are in orderly display along the wall opposite the windows.

Each of the learning centers in this classroom has a filmstrip projector. The center directions are neatly presented on cards. The task cards are color coded by activities. Many posters, charts, and pictures are available. A large wall map is present. The chalkboard is divided into sections by content and contains examples in colored chalk. The teacher makes frequent use of an overhead projector.

Much instruction takes place from the teacher's desk. Workbooks, worksheets, and pictorial presentations dominate instruction. Reading is frequently done silently, stressing a sight word approach. Configuration and pictures are used as clues for unlocking new words. Math drill is either from worksheets or flashcards. Spelling is practiced through the use of flashcards. Instructions to the children are often in the form of task cards or printed materials. Art activities are common, usually two-dimensional, with line, color, and shape stressed.

The students are required to obtain permission to talk or move about the room. Responding to printed material is frequent. Slide films and movies are viewed to provide instruction or as special activity. Coloring and picture making are encouraged for open activity periods. Written work is common.

The three classrooms described above may be at the same grade level, in the same building, and separated only by a shared hallway. What is most surprising, the teachers in the three classrooms may have no idea why they prefer their classrooms that way.

The three classrooms reflect the teachers' styles far more than the children's styles. Teachers, just like students, are individuals and differ from one another. One of the ways that these differences are evident is through a teacher's classroom organization. It is clear that Room 113 will be received better by an auditory learner than will either Room 114 or 115. For the visual learner, Room 115 represents the most positive environment. Note however, that one classroom is not better for all children than either of the other two. One classroom is better for the child whose modality strength is consistent with the organization of the classroom, which is determined in great part by the modality strength of the teacher.

*Research supports the contention that modality-based instruction works.* Although we would like to be able to report that research unequivocally supports modality-based instruction, no such unequivocal support exists. Experts are sharply divided on whether or not modality-based instruction works, and the controversy surrounding the topic continues.

A summary of the research on teaching reading through learner modality strengths was conducted by Tarver and Dawson (1978), who reviewed fifteen studies published within a ten year period. They wrote:

> In summary, the evidence indicates conclusively that modality preference and method of teaching reading do not interact significantly when we are concerned with actual methods of teaching reading and measures of reading achievement rather than listening tasks and measures of recall or recognition (Tarver and Dawson, 1978, p. 20).

Although the Tarver and Dawson review is quite clear in its conclusion, it should be noted that, in the studies they reviewed, there is a problem about the identification of the modality strengths of the subjects involved. Our research, and that of others, suggests that modality strengths may change over time during the elementary school years, and that the proportions of visual, auditory, kinesthetic, and mixed modality learners are not equal. Thus, by simply dividing a group of students at the median or some other convenient point and saying one group is high in a specific modality while the other is low does not guarantee that any real difference exists between the groups. The dividing point may change from year to year, and will vary from modality to modality. The identification of learners with a specific modality strength is therefore problematic, and if this identification was done incorrectly, the lack of an interaction between modality strength and teaching method is not so much an indictment of modality-specific teaching as of the process used to classify subjects according to their modality strengths.

Another shortcoming of the Tarver and Dawson review relates to the treatment conditions reported in the studies. Instead of being systematic applications of a consistent procedure, the teaching methods or interventions described lack comprehensiveness and consistency, or are inconsequential. The interventions may have failed in their purpose not because they were based on a faulty theory, but because they were poorly designed interventions.

Finally, the conclusion drawn by Tarver and Dawson is not the only one that the data support. Depending upon one's orientation, either twelve or thirteen of the studies they reviewed showed no interaction between modality strengths and teaching method. Tarver and Dawson interpreted this as a failure of modality-based instruction, but a contradictory conclusion can be drawn. The following analogy will clarify this point.

Suppose that fifteen races were held to compare gasoline-powered automobiles with vehicles powered by electricity. The gasoline-powered vehicles won twelve of the races, so the conclusion was that electric vehicles were not feasible. The inventors of the electric car, however, drew the opposite conclusion and were encouraged by the results of the race. They felt that, considering the long development period of gasoline-powered automobile engines and the comparatively primitive state of the art of electrically powered vehicles, the three victories suggested that the electric car could potentially compete with standard gasoline-powered vehicles.

When you apply this analogy to the Tarver and Dawson review, the three instances of the expected interaction can be construed as support for modality-based instruction. Although modality-based instruction has a long history, it has never been pursued consistently. Therefore, when contrasted with more conventional instructional approaches, it is prototypical. Yet, even in this comparatively immature state, it proved superior to conventional instruction 20 percent of the time. We see this finding as encouraging, and as the methods and materials of modality-based instruction are improved, we anticipate an increase in the proportion of cases in which modality-based instruction proves superior to more conventional approaches.

The Tarver and Dawson review, although intended to refute the effectiveness of modality-based instruction, can be interpreted as indirect support for the practice. The following comments are offered as direct support for teaching through modality strengths.

In his development of the Learning Methods Test, Mills found that "different children learn to recognize words more efficiently by different teaching methods and that no one method is best for all children"

(Mills, 1970, p. 56). The controls Mills used in his study were not the most stringent, but his methods were sufficiently sound to warrant our use of his results as evidence supporting modality-based instruction.

Mozingo (1978), in the review of the literature that set the stage for her dissertation, cited a study conducted by Fry in 1969. In this study, a group of first grade students with a predominant auditory modality acquired better silent reading skills when taught using a phonetic approach than when a visual approach was used. Fry's finding was corroborated by the results of Mozingo's (1978) dissertation, in which elementary school students with an auditory preference demonstrated better immediate and delayed recall of a list of memorized words presented to them in their strongest modality. Visually oriented students evidenced superior immediate retention of visually presented words; no such superiority emerged with delayed recall.

This evidence substantiates the contention that modality-based education works. Even the Tarver and Dawson (1978) review, which may be viewed as refuting the matching of teaching strategies with students' modality strengths, can be construed as indirect support for modality-based education, or at least its potential. The comment that best summarizes the effectiveness of modality-based education appeared in an article on learning styles, in which the authors stated that "extensive observations and research verify significant improvement in both student achievement and motivation when learning and teaching styles are matched" (Dunn and Dunn, 1979, p. 242).

## Fundamentals of Modality-Based Instruction

Teaching to modality strengths is a readily understandable concept. All it entails is that teachers present a lesson in such a way that students can apply their learning strengths to understanding the material. Generally speaking, there is no need for teachers to revamp entirely their teaching strategies. Through comparatively minor curriculum modifications, most lessons can be adapted in such a way that visual, auditory, and kinesthetic learners can benefit from the lesson.

There are occasions when a particular learner may not understand a lesson as the teacher first presents it. This is called the *point of intervention*. At this point it is necessary for the teacher to personalize instruction. He or she must either group that child with others who have similar strengths, or direct the child to material that utilizes his or her learning strength.

Modality-based teaching, the point of intervention, and personalized instruction will be discussed further in a subsequent chapter. We have introduced these concepts at the present time as a preface to our discussion of the two foundations of modality-based instruction. The first of these is that the teacher must know his or her own modality strength, and the second is that the teacher must be cognizant of the modality strengths of each student.

*Knowing one's own modality strength.* Most adults are vaguely aware of the modalities through which they learn best. Such a vague awareness is not sufficient for teachers, however, since they tend to project their own modality strengths into their selection of materials, teaching strategies and procedures, and methods of reinforcement. In other words, we teach as we learn best, not as we were taught.

Consider, for instance, the primary grade teacher who is highly auditory. The natural tendency of this teacher is to stress phonics as the best, and perhaps the only way to attack new words. What could be more natural than teaching a sound-symbol relationship as a means of learning to read? The method worked for the teacher when he or she learned to read, has strong support in the professional literature, and provides the teacher with the opportunity to organize a lesson around his or her area of strength. As the teacher expected, most of the class (those who are auditory or who are auditory in combination with one of the other modalities) learned the skills associated with the phonics method. The remainder of the class had more difficulty using phonics to learn new words, but the teacher continues to hope that with more practice, they will indeed learn appropriate word attack skills.

Obviously, the auditory teacher will lean heavily on the phonics approach, and the auditory child will benefit. Conversely, the non-auditory teacher, one who is primarily visual or kinesthetic, will minimize the importance of the sound-symbol relationship, and the auditory child will receive fewer of the benefits of a phonics approach. The non-auditory teacher may attempt to follow the lesson plan outlined in the teachers' guide, and yet unintentionally miss the subtleties of the lesson, perhaps even mishearing the sounds the children are making. After several years of frustration, the non-auditory teacher will drift away from phonics instruction altogether, and become convinced of the futility of using the approach. To the non-auditory teacher, phonics just does not work.

Much the same is true of other instructional approaches. Montessori-type methods are favored by kinesthetic teachers, while visual teachers prefer approaches that depend upon the recognition of words by their configuration. Almost always, teachers tend to prefer methods that involve their own modality strength. There is nothing wrong with this practice, so long as teachers are flexible enough to change their method when it does not work.

Parenthetically, we would like to add that no teacher is more in need of understanding his or her modality strength than the kinesthetic teacher. The chief reason for this need is that there are so few kinesthetic teachers. Other than in coaching and teaching kindergarten, kinesthetic skills are not seen in a positive light. Kinesthetic teachers in the regular elementary classroom tend to have classrooms in which there seems to be little organization, primarily because out-of-seat activities are favored by this teacher. Auditory and visual teachers look upon the activity in the kinesthetic teacher's classroom with disdain. If principals and supervisors evidence similar disdain, then the kinesthetic teacher may be discouraged from pursuing education as a profession. The teacher who realizes that he or she is kinesthetic will understand why there are so few teachers with similar teaching styles in the school, why some other teachers complain of his or her disordered classroom, and why supervisors and principals are reluctant to rate his or her work as superior. Kinesthetic teachers are neither better nor worse than teachers with other modality strengths, but because their teaching strategies are not always in line with commonly accepted practices, they are sometimes misunderstood by their colleagues.

*Knowing the modality strengths of each student.* The chief reason that teachers need to be aware of the modality strengths of the students for whom they have responsibility is that instruction can then be organized around those strengths. Instructional methods and materials that are consistent with the modality strengths of students have a greater likelihood of success, and are often more enjoyable to both students and teachers. There is no rule that says that education has to be painful.

Teachers should be aware of three aspects of the modality characteristics of their students:

1. the modality through which each child learns best,
2. the modalities that are not effective for instruction,
3. the modalities that interfere with learning.

The first two points are easily understood; the third requires some elaboration.

When information is presented in more than one modality, most children have little difficulty understanding the message. They either focus on the message transmitted through one modality or integrate the multiple stimuli into a single message. Some children are unable to do this, however, and the presence of parallel stimulation prevents learning. A teacher who knows which children are subject to this problem, and who can identify the circumstances under which interference takes place, will have an easier time reaching the child than a teacher who is not aware of this interference.

## Conclusion

A historical note from more than fifty years ago summarizes well the view of modality we are advocating in this book. In a discussion of imagination, Myers pointed out that in recollecting a rose,

> . . . we saw the rose, smelled the rose, felt ourselves plucking it, handling it, or tasting it . . . in an attempt to recall that particular rose. Consequently, the notion grew up of types, such as visiles, audiles, and motiles, or those who recalled in terms of how the thing looks or sounds or in terms of their feelings of moving in relation to it and handling it.

Myers goes on to state that

> . . . images which the average individual gets in recall, though one type may prevail, are of a variety of kinds, and that, therefore, we should make a variety of sensory appeals in teaching (1925, pp. 197–198).

We are not promoting a ''shotgun'' approach to education through the indiscriminate use of multisensory materials, nor are we implying that teachers should rely exclusively on a single modality. A teacher's awareness of modality strengths should serve as the framework within which effective instruction can take place. Such an awareness will encourage the curriculum modifications that will benefit students, and will help the teacher avoid forcing his or her own modality strength on a student. In addition, when it appears that a student has not grasped a lesson as it is first presented, knowledge of that student's modality strength can serve as the basis for a change in the manner of presentation.

# References

Dunn, R.S. and Dunn, K.J. Learning styles/teaching styles: should they . . . can they . . . be matched? *Educational Leadership,* 1979, *36,* 238–244.

Epstein, W. *Varieties of perceptual learning.* New York: McGraw-Hill, 1967.

Fry, E. Comparison of beginning reading with i.t.a., DMS, and t.o. after three years. *The Reading Teacher,* 1969, *22,* 357–362.

Klatzky, R.L. *Human memory: structures and processes.* San Francisco: Freeman, 1975.

Mills, R.E. *The teaching of word recognition.* Ft. Lauderdale: The Mills School, 1970.

Mozingo, L.L. *An investigation of auditory and visual modality preferences for teaching word recognition skills to students classified as auditory or visual learners.* Doctoral dissertation, University of South Carolina, 1978.

Myers, G.C. *The learner and his attitude.* New York: Sanborn, 1925.

Tarver, S.G. and Dawson, M.M. Modality preference and the teaching of reading: a review. *Journal of Learning Disabilities,* 1978, *11,* 17–29.

Wepman, J.M. Modalities and learning. In H.M. Robinson (Ed.), *Coordinating reading instruction.* Glenview, Ill.: Scott Foresman, 1971.

# CHAPTER II

# The History of Modality-Based Instruction

The antecedents of today's modality-based instruction are the focus of this chapter. Not surprisingly, auditory, visual, and kinesthetic methods of teaching reading and writing have a history almost as old as that of the written word itself. Following this discussion will be a commentary on why modality-based instruction has not yet received the support of educators its history would merit.

Efforts to teach writing and reading through the auditory, visual, and kinesthetic modalities have been documented since pre-Christian Greece (Fernald, 1943). Before the advent of writing, the spoken word was the principal means by which information was transmitted from person to person and from generation to generation. Logically enough, when writing appeared upon the scene, auditory methods were first used to teach its complement, reading. Hence, the phonetic method was a legacy from the ancient Greeks and Romans, who taught reading by sounding words.

It is of interest to note that writing was greeted less than enthusiastically by some prominent Greeks. They feared that reliance upon writing would cause atrophy of the mind, and that memorization would become a lost art.

Young Romans were taught to read through the visual-auditory method; they said aloud words or letters while looking at a printed copy of the words or letters. This method also served as the basis for textbooks used in England and the Colonies during the seventeenth century. Printed names of objects, sometimes accompanied by representations of the objects themselves, were associated with letters of the alphabet. Students would recite the word, its initial letter, and a short rhyme using the word in context.

Kinesthetic methods akin to those used even today had a place in education since before the birth of Christ. The Greeks taught writing by tracing with a stylus or by guiding a child's hand through the movements corresponding to the shape of a letter. The same methods were used by the Romans, who added a new twist. By cutting letters into wax tablets, the child could trace the shape of each letter unerringly. While tracing, the student was encouraged to learn the sounds of the letters. Finally, carved letters were developed. These three-dimensional representations were manipulated by the child while an adult or the child repeated the sound of each letter.

For an obvious reason, the teaching techniques described above persisted with few changes through the Middle Ages. Education was almost exclusively a privilege of the upper class or those with a religious vocation; given this constraint, it was unnecessary to experiment with alternative approaches. Should the scion of a noble family fail to learn his lessons, it was much less trouble to enlist the services of a scholar than to change the teaching process. With respect to future clerics, failure to acquire reading and writing skills meant either that the person had no real vocation, or that common labor in a monastery was the manner in which that person was meant to serve God best.

As the middle class amassed more wealth and power in the post-Renaissance period, the pool of potential students increased, necessitating certain changes in didactic techniques. Further, during the Age of Enlightenment, intellectuals discussed the true nature of man and the possibility of extending the rights of the lower classes. At the same time these discussions were taking place, the lower classes themselves were engaged in a somewhat more active pursuit of their rights. The American and French revolutions were soon to occur and the time was ripe for educational innovation.

It is important to keep in mind that although kinesthetic methods were available to teach basic skills, there was a decided preference for visual and auditory methods based on memorization. Where this prejudice had its start is unclear, but there seemed to be a belief, much as there is today, that rote learning is superior to any method that calls upon the kinesthetic or combined modalities. Repetition and reliance upon auditory and visual stimuli were *de rigueur* in the mid-eighteenth century classroom.

Into this environment came three men whose ideas would greatly influence the course of education. Jean Jacques Rousseau, an extremist proponent of natural education, argued that sense experience was the basis for all knowledge. He stressed the importance of an awareness of the characteristics of the individual and emphasized the process of learning rather than what was learned. His contemporary, Jacob Rod-riquez Pereira, a Spaniard, was of like mind. More practically oriented than Rousseau, Pereira was engaged in actual teaching. His work with deaf children followed upon his belief that the kinesthetic or tactile senses served as the basis for the functioning of all the other senses (Kramer, 1976).

Etienne Bonnot de Condillac, a French philosopher of the sensa-tionalist school, stated that the key to education was in taking control of the child's sensory experience, of directing and developing it (Lane, 1976). Since children manifested a great deal of variety in their sensory characteristics, it was necessary to observe the child closely in order that an individualized program of instruction could be developed.

Around the close of the eighteenth century, the ideas of Rousseau, Condillac, and Pereira were applied by several educators of note. Johan Pestalozzi, influenced by Rousseau, started a school to train impov-erished and neglected children in a rural area of Switzerland (Kramer, 1976). Later put in charge of other schools, Pestalozzi promoted the doctrine of training the senses. He organized the activities in his schools in such a way that students progressed from the simple to the complex, and from the concrete to the abstract.

Friedrich Froebel, a disciple of Pestalozzi, was disenchanted with the rigidity and routine that characterized his mentor's schools, and opened his own school. Froebel sought to stimulate learning through play, and coined the term *kindergarten* to describe the environment where children could grow like flowers (Kramer, 1976). Froebel's schools eventually closed or failed, but his banner was taken up by others, and kindergartens soon flourished in other countries.

Condillac's sensationalism had a great impact on a young Paris physician, Jean Marc Gaspard Itard. Appointed resident physician at the Institute for Deaf-Mutes, Itard took up the training of the Wild Boy of Aveyron, a feral child who had been found in the forests of south central France almost a year before.

The task set before Itard was no mean feat. Phillipe Pinel, the then leading authority on mental disorders, described the child as "suffering from idiocy and insanity" and being without hope of "obtaining some measure of success through systematic and continued instruction" (Lane, 1976, p. 69). The chances of making the child literate and socially acceptable were remote.

Itard was strongly influenced by the belief of Rousseau and Condillac that the stimulation of the senses was essential to all other learning. Such an approach was fine in theory, but the philosophers failed to provide him with practical guidance. Itard turned to the experiences of the Abbe de Sicard, a noted teacher of deaf children and Director of the Institute.

Sicard's work with Jean Massieu, a child deaf since birth, was acclaimed throughout France. In teaching Massieu, Sicard relied upon the kinesthetic and visual modalities; he had no other recourse, since his pupil had no usable hearing. The teacher first instructed the child how to match familiar objects with their drawn outlines. The printed name of the object was soon included with the outline; later, the outline would be removed and Massieu would match the objects with their printed or written names. Massieu proved to be an exceptional learner, and under the tutelage of Sicard, progressed further than anyone thought possible.

Encouraged by the success of Sicard, Itard began his work with Victor, the *enfant sauvage*. The child seemed to be endowed with certain highly developed visual, auditory, and manipulative faculties; it was upon these faculties that Itard hoped to build. He set to teaching Victor in the same way as Sicard did with Massieu, by matching familiar objects with their outlines. The child was slow to catch on, but after several false starts, soon acquired some facility in the task. The first step toward mastering necessary skills had been taken.

As the next step, Victor learned to match simple geometric shapes— a circle, a triangle, and a square—to their outlines. He learned to make finer and finer distinctions based on these three basic shapes, prompting Itard to begin discrimination training in other modalities.

After discrimination skills had been firmly established, Itard devised an intermediate step to bridge the gap between discrimination of shapes and letter recognition. Itard used a compositor's table on which Victor could match a sample sequence of letters by inserting individual letters into a frame. Although the child seemed to learn the task, it was some time before he made the conceptual leap of associating the letters in the frame with objects in the room or his favorite foods.

Through numerous exercises involving all the senses, particularly the kinesthetic, Victor acquired the rudiments of language. A description of these activities is presented by Lane (1976) in his definitive treatment of the training of the Wild Boy. Unfortunately, the episodes of hysteria to which Victor was subject, resembling the experimental neurosis Pavlov was to stumble upon later that century, prevented Itard's continuing work with the boy.

While still working with Victor, Itard commented that the progress of education would best be fostered by "detecting the organic and intellectual peculiarities of each individual and determining therefrom what education ought to do" (Lane, 1976, p. 130). Thus, he advocated the personalization of instruction, and promoted reliance upon the sensory or modality strengths of each student. Itard may have failed in his efforts to socialize Victor, but in trying, he developed techniques and materials that served as the stepping stones to success for later educators.

Itard continued his career as a teacher by working with deaf children; later, he agreed to direct Eduard Seguin in educating mentally retarded children. Seguin adapted Itard's methods to this population and focused on the development of the senses, beginning with the kinesthetic. Motor coordination was seen as the first necessary skill, with tactile discrimination following. Visual training proceeded next, with the initial goal being to gain control of eye movements. This served as a prelude to making discriminations. Finally, auditory and speech training were undertaken. The final step would occur only after the stronger modalities had been thoroughly trained.

If there was one shortcoming of Itard's methodology, it was that it could be used only on a one-to-one basis. Seguin overcame this and was able to train large numbers of retarded children. An even wider application of Itard's work would occur in the next century with the work of Maria Montessori.

Maria Montessori trained as a medical doctor, but soon after completing her studies was taken with the plight of the disadvantaged children of Rome. After studying the works of Seguin, Itard, and Pereira, she became convinced that mentally retarded and emotionally disturbed children, children with other handicaps, and especially the children of poor working class families could benefit from an education. The methods she developed to accomplish this purpose resulted in more than simply the education of these children: they brought her work international recognition.

The techniques formulated by Montessori carried on the tradition founded by Itard of teaching through knowledge of physiology: first educate the senses, then educate the intellect (Kramer, 1976). The didactic materials that she designed were self-correcting and "auto-educational,'' and were intended to provide for the comfort of the child as well as to promote sensory and motoric development (Montessori, 1912).

All of the educationally relevant senses were tapped through Montessori's approach. The sequence involved can roughly be described in the following manner:

1. Through sensory stimulation, the child will gain perceptual skills.
2. Once these skills have been mastered, increasingly subtle discriminations can be made.
3. Gradually, the transition from purely sensory materials such as shapes and blocks to three-dimensional representations of letters will be brought about.
4. Recognition of letters, combined with other kinesthetic activities, will lead to writing, soon to be followed by reading.

The teacher's role in the Montessori method is akin to that of a guide. By methodically observing a student engaged in spontaneous play, the teacher can gain an understanding of the student's learning strengths (Montessori, 1912; 1914). Materials are provided to capitalize upon these strengths, the natural curiosity of the child, and the penchant children have for activity. Montessori felt that making these materials available to children would result in the spontaneous acquisition of pre-academic and academic skills. There is little doubt that to Montessori, things were the best teachers (Kramer, 1976).

Montessori and her followers used visual and auditory materials, to be sure, but they leaned most heavily upon the tactile and kinesthetic. The emphasis upon tactile and kinesthetic materials followed from the seminal tenet of the Montessori method, the liberty of the pupil (Kramer, 1976). By removing the physical constraints that were traditionally associated with classroom instruction, and by replacing them with activities that revolved around the sensory and motor capabilities of the students, the unhindered physical and psychological growth of the child would be fostered.

The successes achieved by Montessori and her followers were without parallel in the history of education. Soon, Montessori became a celebrity in Italy; later, she would be hailed throughout the Continent and in America. And yet, within five years of her death, both she and her methods would be almost forgotten.

The chief reason that Montessori's methods passed into obsolescence is outlined by her biographer, Rita Kramer:

> . . . the movement became isolated from the newly developing currents of thought that were influencing the most creative European psychologists and educators just as in America it had become cut off from the mainstream of development in those fields and remained drifting in the backwaters of a few private schools (1976, p. 377).

By ignoring the three new paths of contemporary psychology—behaviorism, psychoanalysis, and psychological testing—Montessori and her supporters brought about the demise of the movement they had nurtured for so many years. As Kramer puts it, "nothing is as inimical to the pursuit of truth as the conviction that one has already found it" (1976, p. 378).

Soon after Montessori had promulgated her methods throughout England and the Continent, Grace Fernald's work began in America. Like Montessori and others before her, Fernald focused her efforts on atypical students: those with physical disabilities and other problems that prevented their learning basic academic skills.

In the Clinic School at the University of California at Los Angeles and at several other sites, Fernald developed an eclectic approach to remediation consisting of two stages:

Stage 1.

> The word is written for the child with crayola on paper in plain blackboard-size script, or in print, if manuscript writing is used. The child traces the word with finger contact, saying each part of the word as he traces it. He repeats this process as many times as necessary in order to write the word without looking at the copy. He writes the word once on scrap paper and then in his "story." After a story has been written by the child, it is typed for him and he reads it in print.

Stage 2.

> This stage is the same as Stage 1, except that tracing is no longer necessary (Fernald, 1943, pp. 35-39).

Fernald identified several key elements of her method, without which success would be unlikely. First, she emphasized that tracing must be undertaken with a finger rather than a stylus or pencil. Finger contact, she felt, was as important to the retention of the word as were the large and small muscle movements by which the tracing was accomplished.

Second, the word must be written as a unit without looking at the original, and each time the word is written, the student must say the word either to himself or aloud. By so doing, three sensory modes are stimulated: the kinesthetic as it is written or copied, the visual as the written word appears on the paper or chalkboard, and the auditory as the word is spoken or subvocalized.

Finally, whatever is written by the child must be used in context, typed for the child, and read by the child before too long an interval passes. The first of these activities ensures that the child will acquire the meaning of the word, while the second and third promote reading from printed material.

One of the components of the Fernald method that is treated almost as an afterthought is perhaps the most reinforcing activity for the kinesthetic or kinesthetic/visual learner. Once a word has been written, the child files the word alphabetically in a word file. If the word file is physically removed from the child, then the very action of walking to the file and placing the card under the appropriate letter will reinforce the correct writing of the word. At the same time, a visual association between the word and its initial letter is established.

The remedial method used by Fernald seemed to work for both children and adults, and for those whose reading disability ranged from total to mild. The method could be used with individual students, but Fernald herself felt that the most satisfactory results were obtained with children working in small groups (Fernald, 1943).

A contemporary of Fernald, Samuel T. Orton, developed techniques to ameliorate the reading, writing, and speech problems of school students. Orton's work received less recognition in educational circles than did Fernald's for two reasons. First, Orton, like Itard and Montessori, was a physician; unlike his medical predecessors, however, he confined most of his work to clinical practice, treating a comparatively small number of students. Second, Orton placed a great deal of emphasis upon brain structure and functioning. The neurological basis for his work was neither readily accepted nor understood by the average teacher.

Several characteristics of Orton's approach merit the notice of today's educators. Most importantly, he acknowledged the essential role of the modalities in everyday functioning. To Orton, our dominant position in the animal world rested largely on the possession of two faculties, speech and manual dexterity (Orton, 1937). Further, although man's eyesight is not so well developed as that of many lower animals, it is the primary means by which information is gathered from the environment.

Orton felt that the relative part played by each of the three major modalities varies markedly in different persons. Consistent with this belief, he suggested that teachers and other remedial specialists should learn the comparative modality strengths of their students.

Finally, to Orton's way of thinking, if one modality was weak, it was necessary to capitalize upon the other, stronger modalities. He identified methods of teaching to modality strengths when specific disabilities were present, and concluded that

> . . . disorders should respond to specific training if we become sufficiently keen in our diagnosis and if we prove ourselves clever enough to devise the proper training methods to meet the needs of each particular case (Orton, 1937, p. 200).

From the late 1940s to the mid 1950s, the cause of modality-based instruction was championed by Strauss, Lehtinen, and Kephart. Their approach to treating learning problems underwent something of an evolution during these years, but they maintained the importance of modality-based learning throughout.

Strauss and Lehtinen (1947) contended that the education of brain-injured children should revolve around three practices: limiting distractions, using motor activities, and promoting independent work. Limiting distractions meant keeping the number of materials and decorations in the classroom at a minimum. The logic behind this practice was that the perception of the brain-injured child is more easily subject to disturbance by external influences. Keeping these disturbances at a minimum would allow the child to learn through only one modality at a time.

They also insisted that lessons and activities should include motor activities. By so doing, the teacher allows the child to engage in the manipulative tendencies manifested by nearly all children. Further, the addition of kinesthetic perception to the other two educationally relevant modalities seems to help bind them into an integrated whole (Strauss and Kephart, 1955).

Promoting independent work, a practice initiated by Montessori, was one upon which Strauss, Lehtinen, and Kephart also leaned heavily. By designing materials that enable a child to work alone, independence is nurtured and teachers are freed to work individually with other students.

Strauss and his associates seemed to feel that vision was the most important sensory mode, but that learning came about, to a great extent, through motility, exploratory behavior, or the curiosity of the child (Strauss and Kephart, 1955). They also implied that the integration of the modalities progresses with age. When the child is very young, the modalities function more or less independently. As the child matures, the modalities are integrated, and perceptions in one modality trigger parallel images in the brain that correspond to those in the other modalities.

Kephart (1960), in commenting on modern society, touched upon an important aspect of modality-based education. He stressed that sensory motor or perceptual motor manipulation was necessary to allow the child to fit his behavior to the changing demands of the contemporary environment. Yet, while civilization increased the demands it placed on the child, it decreased the opportunities offered to the child to experiment with basic skills. Thus, Kephart was reiterating Montessori's position that sensory motor activities were the basis for later academic and survival skills, and that this held true for all children, not just those with learning problems.

Modality-based education has almost always been associated with special education; in the 1960s, it was seen as a potentially effective strategy for working with learning disabled children. Samuel Kirk popularized this belief, arguing that the language problems that impeded the learning of reading and writing had a perceptual basis. He developed the Illinois Test of Psycholinguistic Abilities (ITPA) (Kirk et al., 1961; 1968; Kirk and Kirk, 1971) to identify these perceptual deficits, and devised methods to remediate them. Kirk coined the term *intraindividual differences* to describe the variations in learning strengths evident in each child. Heretofore, identifying interindividual or between child differences was the primary purpose of educational diagnosis. Through the ITPA, Kirk hoped to develop a profile of each student showing the relative strengths of perceptual skills within each child.

Kirk's approach to remediation consisted of several steps which included:

1. identifying deficient areas;
2. training the deficient areas, remediating prerequisite skills first;
3. utilizing areas of strength;
4. using multisensory presentations selectively.

As is evident from these steps, Kirk's methods were a form of modality-based instruction.

Within a few years of Kirk's development of the ITPA, Marianne Frostig published a program to facilitate the development of visual perception (Frostig and Horne, 1964). This program was meant to be both corrective and preventive, and reflected Frostig's belief that vision was the most important modality. The Frostig program comprised five elements: perception of position in space; perception of spatial relationships; perception of constancy; visual-motor coordination; and figure ground perception. Students were trained in visual-motor coordination of the upper and lower limbs, eye movement exercises were prescribed, and both gross and fine muscle activities were encouraged.

The materials developed by Frostig had two features that were unique. First, she devised a comparatively simple means of assessing the components of visual perception. Unfortunately, her assessment tool focused attention on the child's deficits. The second unique feature of her method was that her interventions could be used in the classroom or in the daily home routine of the child. The latter feature allowed developmental and remedial tasks to be practiced for a much greater length of time than are purely classroom oriented tasks.

By the 1970s, although the target population for modality-based instruction was still primarily those with special problems, the multisensory approach was beginning to receive attention in general education. No tidal wave of support for modality-based instruction swept through the education profession, but a ground swell of support was building. R. E. Mills published the Learning Methods Test (1970), the Swassing-Barbe Modality Index was in its incipient stages, and Rita and Kenneth Dunn were building the Learning Style Inventory (1975). Modality was not yet a common term, but it was becoming more frequently heard in educational circles.

## Commentary

Given the long and rich history evidenced by modality-based instruction, it is surprising that teaching strategies based on all the educationally relevant modalities have not become an integral part of contemporary schooling. The progress of modality-based education has paralleled the course of education in general, but has never risen

above the status of a recurrent fad. Several factors have contributed to this situation.

First, there is a certain air of superiority associated with being able to recite from memory material presented either auditorily or visually. Combined methods, or those that rely upon the kinesthetic modality, are seen as recourses to be turned to only when all else has failed. This attitude may be a throwback to the time when word of mouth was the only means of transmitting information from person to person, and rote memory was necessary to ensure the continuance of the species.

The second factor is a corollary of the first: modality-based education has acquired the connotation of being remedial. Despite the exhortations of Montessori and Frostig that normal development requires sensorimotor stimulation, and despite the arguments of Rousseau and Condillac for universal education built upon our knowledge of the senses, modality-based education has primarily been used as a special education tool since the beginning of the nineteenth century. Remarkable results have been obtained with both handicapped and normal learners, but the principles of modality-based education have been accepted only hesitatingly.

Third, there were few materials available by which to assess the comparative modality strengths of individual learners. Itard and Montessori leaned heavily upon observation, but left no practical guidelines by which others could learn their techniques. The psychological tests upon which Fernald, Strauss, Lehtinen, and Kephart relied are not within the competency repertoire of classroom teachers, since their use is limited to certified or licensed psychologists. Kirk's ITPA requires a good deal of time and training for proper administration. Frostig's material focused only on visual perception and was deficit oriented. The Mill's Learning Methods Test, which is appropriate for classroom use, requires so much time for administration that its value is limited. Without some practical means of assessing the perceptual strengths of individual learners, a modality-based approach to education is impossible.

Finally, with the exception of the approach developed by Maria Montessori, no curriculum based on teaching to modality strengths has been developed. For the most part, efforts to instruct students in accordance with their sensory strengths have been directed at remediating a specific deficit or teaching an individual skill. No framework has been available within which teachers could organize their everyday teaching activities.

## References

Dunn, R.S. and Dunn, K.J. *Learning Style Inventory*. Lawrence, Kan.: Price Systems, 1975.

Fernald, G.M. *Remedial techniques in basic school subjects*. New York: McGraw-Hill, 1943.

Frostig, M. and Horne, D. *The Frostig program for the development of visual perception*. Chicago: Follett, 1964.

Kephart, N.C. *The slow learner in the classroom*. Columbus, Ohio: Merrill, 1960.

Kirk, S.A. and Kirk, W.D. *Psycholinguistic learning disabilities: diagnosis and remediation*. Urbana: University of Illinois, 1971.

Kirk, S.A.; McCarthy, J.J.; and Kirk, W.D. *Illinois Test of Psycholinguistic Abilities (Experimental Edition)*. Urbana: University of Illinois, 1961.

———. *Illinois Test of Psycholinguistic Abilities*. Urbana: University of Illinois, 1968.

Kramer, R. *Maria Montessori*. New York: Putnam, 1976.

Lane, H. *The wild boy of Aveyron*. Cambridge, Mass.: Harvard University, 1976.

Mills, R.E. *The teaching of word recognition*. Ft. Lauderdale: The Mills School, 1970.

Montessori, M. *The Montessori method*. New York: Stokes, 1912.

———. *Dr. Montessori's own handbook*. New York: Schochen, 1914.

Orton, S.T. *Reading, writing, and speech problems in children*. New York: Norton, 1937.

Strauss, A.A. and Kephart, N.C. *Psychopathology and education of the brain-injured child: Volume II. Progress in theory and clinic*. New York: Grune and Stratton, 1955.

Strauss, A.A. and Lehtinen, L.E. *Psychopathology and education of the brain-injured child*. New York: Grune and Stratton, 1947.

# CHAPTER III

# Identifying Modality Strengths

Before modality-based instruction can begin, the teacher must be able to assess modality strengths. This chapter reviews assessment methods that were used in the past, and presents to the reader the Swassing-Barbe Modality Index (SBMI). The development and use of the SBMI are discussed, as are observational methods that supplement the SBMI.

## Introduction

The goal of educational testing should be to sensitize the teacher to a particular skill, ability, or strength of a student. Unfortunately, the testing movement in the United States has lost sight of this goal, and has emphasized weaknesses, deficiencies, and problem areas. Intelligence testing is a good example of this trend.

Intelligence tests often comprise tasks that are indices of learning strengths; a child's performance on these tasks can give a teacher a good idea of the circumstances under which a child learns best. Yet, the score on an intelligence test is most often used to determine the limit of a child's potential. Instead of fostering growth, intelligence tests have too often been used to stifle it.

This need not be the case, for an intelligence quotient, rather than being viewed exclusively as a ceiling, is better seen as a base. Scores on an intelligence test would indicate that on a particular day, with a particular examiner, and under particular conditions, the child could perform at least that well. Under more favorable conditions, in the classroom for example, the child can be expected to do even better. Further, when interpreted properly, the results of an intelligence test can be used by a teacher to expand the learning potential of students.

In order to avoid the pitfalls that have characterized the use of intelligence tests and other instruments, the Swassing-Barbe Modality Index (SBMI) has been designed to be strength oriented. That is, it

31

identifies the modalities through which the child learns best. Once these strengths have been identified, instruction can be organized to capitalize upon them.

Another characteristic of the SBMI is that the results of the test are reported in percentages. Thus, modality strengths are relative within the child; comparisons between children are meaningless. One child is neither better nor worse than other children, only different.

The SBMI, like any measurement tool, is simply a behavioral sample that is intended to predict the manner in which the child will function in real life or academic situations. Although the SBMI can stand alone, we recommend that it be used in conjunction with teacher observations. It is our belief that careful observation by a sensitive adult is the best way to identify a child's modality strength. The SBMI can, however, supplement these observations by providing a structured situation in which the child is called upon to function using each modality.

## Previous Efforts at Assessing Modality Strengths

The earliest efforts to identify the channels through which children learn best were purely observational. Rousseau and Condillac, in the middle of the eighteenth century, implied that observing very young children, or perhaps primitive adults who had not yet been influenced by civilization, could provide clues as to the true nature of the human species. Once the essential features of the species were identified, educational practices could be initiated to promote the development of the species as nature intended it.

The rhetoric of Rousseau and Condillac had its first practical application at the hands of Itard. Before attempting to instruct Victor, the feral child who was placed in his charge, Itard spent a good deal of time observing the child and reviewing the observations of others. Based on the information he acquired, Itard developed activities intended to teach the basic skills required of a civilized and literate person.

Montessori also relied upon observation to develop the teaching methods for which she is acclaimed. When pressed to disclose the most important skill she required of her teachers, she was quick to reply, ''this is what the teacher must know, how to observe'' (Montessori, 1914, p. 14).

The first effort to assess modality strength through a structured activity was made by Seguin. He used a form board consisting of three shapes: a square, a triangle, and a circle. The child was instructed to insert each shape in the appropriate place on the form board. If difficulty was encountered in completing this task, remedial activities were undertaken before more complex discriminations were attempted.

In the latter part of the nineteenth century, Binet and Simon were commissioned by the French government to develop a means of identifying those children who could not benefit from public education. Several of the procedures they used to accomplish this task, among which were memorizing series of digits and matching patterns of beads, were primarily tests of modality strength. Unfortunately, rather than developing into tests of learning strength, these same activities were incorporated into intelligence tests. Test makers failed to acknowledge that their instruments were measures of learning strengths; the notion that intelligence is a fixed characteristic which can be represented by a single score superseded the more positive and practical aspects of their tests, and the instruments lost much of their value for educators.

Tests that measured individual modality strengths, but were not referred to as such, appeared with regularity during the middle third of the twentieth century. These instruments were deficit oriented, and were aimed at children who required special education, or adults in need of rehabilitation. Among the tests were those that measured visual-motor coordination, auditory processing and memory, small and large muscle coordination.

Although measures of modality strengths have been with us since the late 1800s, it was not until the 1960s that an instrument was designed whose principal purpose was the identification of modality strengths and which provided information on more than a single modality. This instrument was the Illinois Test of Psycholinguistic Abilities (ITPA) (Kirk, et al., 1961; 1968). The ITPA assesses, among other characteristics, visual and auditory processing and retention, and is therefore an advance over previously developed instruments which provided information on only one modality. The ITPA requires extensive training before it can be appropriately administered, and is a very time consuming test. Few classroom teachers have either the time or the training necessary to make practical use of the ITPA.

The Learning Methods Test (Mills, 1970) was the first assessment procedure that tapped all three modalities and their combinations. Developed for use in grades kindergarten through three, the test is based on actually teaching students a set of unknown words through each of the modalities and combinations of modalities. The modality through which the child learns and retains the words most effectively is considered to be the learning strength. The greatest limitation of the Learning Methods Test is the time necessary for its administration. Approximately thirty minutes per day for four days plus a follow-up session are required to administer the test.

Dunn and Dunn (1975) published the Learning Style Inventory, a self-report instrument consisting of 104 true-false items. Each item is answered as it reflects the respondent's personal style. Among the dimensions assessed are what the authors refer to as "perceptual strengths" (Dunn and Dunn, 1979). Since the instrument relies upon perceived strengths and not actual functioning, it is likely that the Learning Style Inventory measures modality preferences rather than modality strengths.

These assessment methods are only a sampling of those that have been used to determine modality strengths; the actual number of such methods is quite extensive. Dechant and Smith (1977), for example, listed thirty-nine separate tests that are commercially available. The ages for which these tests have been developed range from two weeks through adulthood, and the techniques used to determine modality strength vary greatly. In terms of the specific modalities assessed, eleven tests were aimed at audition, thirteen addressed some element or component of vision, five dealt with kinesthesia either alone or in combination with other modalities; the remainder did not clearly fit any category.

## Development of the Swassing-Barbe Modality Index

Given the proliferation of instruments that purport to measure modality strengths, one might well ask if there is a need for yet another one. Considering that most deal only with one modality, extensive time and training are necessary for the administration of many of them, and at least one is based on the questionable practice of equating modality preference with strength, the answer is yes. Classroom teachers are in need of a tool that is practical and yet provides them with information that can serve as the basis for planning instruction around modality strengths.

The Swassing-Barbe Modality Index (SBMI) is an attempt to provide such an instrument. It addresses a variety of needs evinced by classroom teachers, and was developed to conform to the following specifications:

1. Administration time is relatively brief, approximately twenty minutes per student.
2. Neither extensive training nor certification is required for its administration.
3. Modality strengths rather than deficits are identified.
4. The test produces a profile of the relative modality strengths of each subject.
5. The instrument is standardized. That is, the administration of the instrument does not vary from student to student.
6. The stimuli presented to the child are consistent for each of the three modalities.
7. The same response is required for each modality.
8. The instrument has applications both in the classroom and in research settings.

## Description of the SBMI

The SBMI is a matching-to-sample task. In this type of task, a stimulus item or sample is presented, and the respondent is asked to duplicate the sample. Matching-to-sample tasks frequently serve as the basis of educational and psychological tests.

The stimulus items in the SBMI are shapes arranged in sequences of increasing length. The shapes include a circle, square, triangle, and heart. Shape was selected as the relevant dimension or cue because it is not a function of the ability to read. As a consequence, the instrument can be used with preschool age children or children whose first language is not English.

Testing is undertaken three times, once in each educationally relevant modality. There are potentially nine stimulus items in each modality subtest. The first item consists of only a single shape, and serves as a sample item, although it is included in the scoring. The last item is the most complex, and involves nine shapes.

The same sequence of shapes is used to assess each modality. In earlier drafts of the test, a unique sequence of shapes appeared for each modality. This proved to be unnecessarily complex, and added nothing to the reliability of the instrument. With elementary school children, we have found that no learning effect takes place as a result of using the same sequence three times. That is, children fail to remember the sequence from modality to modality.

Stimulus control is an important aspect of the test. As was mentioned previously, the same stimuli are presented in each modality, and all shapes are of the same size, color, and texture. There are no sensory cues other than those intended which could lead students to construct the correct sequence.

## Administration of the SBMI

The SBMI is an individually administered test that normally can be completed in fifteen to twenty minutes. Scoring the test takes only a few minutes, and the interpretation is straightforward.

We recommend strongly that prior to administering the SBMI, the teacher or examiner become thoroughly familiar with the components of the test and the administration procedure. Practicing the administration of the SBMI several times is a very good way to familiarize oneself with the instrument. We have also found it helpful if the administrator first is tested by someone who is experienced with the test. The administrator will then be familiar with the test from the perspective of the student, and will have a better idea of his or her own modality strength.

Just as is true with many educational and psychological assessment tools, the environment in which the SBMI is administered is important. For the comfort of both the administrator and the child, the desk or table on which the testing is conducted should be at least 24 by 36 inches. A larger work surface is preferable; otherwise, the materials not in use must be kept on a chair or table next to the administrator. The scoring sheet and a pencil should be convenient to the tester but not obvious to the child.

If the child is unfamiliar with the person administering the test, it is advisable to establish rapport. Speak briefly with the child, share something about yourself, and ask questions that will encourage the child to be comfortable and relaxed. A favorable testing situation will increase the probability that the child will respond optimally.

When administering the test, sit next to the child on the side of the child's dominant hand. You can often establish handedness by asking the child; if this does not work, hand an object to the child. Most children will reach for the object with their dominant hand.

At this point, empty the envelope of loose shapes in front of the child, leaving approximately an arm's length between the blocks and the child. Begin testing with the visual items. Place the first stimulus item, a circle mounted on a plastic strip, in front of the child and say something to the effect that ''We are going to play a game. I'll show you some shapes. You can look at them until I take them away. After I take the shapes away, you make the same thing using the blocks in front of you.''

Be sure the child understands the procedure, especially when more than one shape is involved. The child must know that simply matching the shapes is not enough; they must be in the same order as the ones you show the child. You may repeat the explanation as often as necessary until you are confident that the child understands. When the testing procedure is clear to the child, continue with the remainder of the items. Present each sequence, allowing the child time to study it. When the sequence contains four or fewer shapes, the child can study the sequence for about ten seconds. When five or more shapes constitute the sequence, permit about twenty seconds. These time limits are not to be adhered to rigidly, so it is advisable to use something less threatening than a stopwatch for timing. Some suggested ways of timing are:

1. Silently count ''One thousand one, one thousand two, one thousand three . . .'' and so on up to ten or twenty, depending upon the length of the sequence involved.
2. Use a clock or watch with a second hand.
3. Use any other method of timing that seems appropriate.

If the child finishes studying the sequence before time is up, take the card away. Otherwise, remove the card from sight at the end of the time limit. The child may begin assembling the pattern as soon as the stimulus sequence is removed. If the child hesitates and says ''I can't remember,'' encourage the child to do the best he or she can and to arrange some of the pattern, if not all of it.

When the child has finished assembling the sequence, compare the response pattern to the appropriate sequence on the record sheet, marking a diagonal line *through those shapes which are placed correctly*. Detailed instructions for scoring responses can be found later in this chapter. When the child makes errors in two consecutive sequences, or completes all the items, stop testing in the visual modality and move to the auditory subtest.

Administer the auditory items by reading aloud the names of the shapes in sequence from the record sheet. The best rate at which to read the shapes is one per second. Lower the pitch of your voice at the last shape to indicate the end of a sequence.

Again, use the first item to explain the procedure. You may introduce the auditory items by saying something like "Now we will go on to another part of the game. This time, I'll read the names of the shapes out loud. Listen carefully, and make the pattern that I say." Be sure that the child does not start reproducing the pattern until you have read the entire sequence.

If there is an interruption during the auditory portion of the SBMI, either while a sequence is being read or while the child is responding, or if the child asks that the sequence be repeated, stop the process and say "Let's try another one." Give the child a moment to prepare, and then read the same sequence aloud but in reverse order. Be sure to score the child's response in the reverse order. The general scoring procedures for the auditory items are the same as for the visual items. When errors occur in two consecutive sequences, or all nine items are completed, proceed to the kinesthetic subtest.

The kinesthetic subtest is administered so that the child can feel the shapes without seeing them. Older children can be instructed to keep their eyes closed. When working with young children, it may be necessary to block their vision so they will not peek at the sequence. The back of the scoring wheel can be used as a shield for this purpose.

Use the first item as an example. Place the stimulus in front of the child, and hold the shield so that the child cannot see the shape. Place the child's dominant hand on the shape, and say "Feel the shapes, and when you are finished, I'll take them away. Then I want you to make the same pattern." The child may use one or both hands to feel the shapes.

For the kinesthetic portion of the test, the child can feel the complete sequence once. As was true with the visual items, allow ten seconds for sequences involving four or fewer shapes, and twenty seconds for sequences longer than four shapes. The child should not be interrupted before he or she has had a chance to feel the whole sequence. If the child accidentally skips a shape, take the child's hand and place it on the missed block. When the child is reconstructing the pattern, she or he is allowed to look at the loose shapes. Continue testing until errors are made in two consecutive sequences or all items are completed.

## Scoring the SBMI

The child's score for each item is the number of shapes that are correctly placed in sequence. There are some types of responses that may prove difficult to score, however, so when these occur, the following guidelines will assist in the scoring process.

1. The first time a reversal of two consecutive shapes occurs anywhere in a subtest, show the child the correct sequence by moving the shapes into the appropriate position, and count the reversed shapes as correct responses. Be sure that the child knows that it is not enough to match the shapes—they must also be in the correct order. All reversals after the first one are to be counted as errors. Indicate all reversals by a double-headed arrow drawn on the scoring sheet between the reversed shapes. Reversals of non-consecutive shapes are always treated as errors.
2. If the child inserts one or more extra shapes in a sequence, ignore the extra shape and score the sequence as if the extra shape had not been included. After the total number of correctly placed shapes for that particular sequence has been tabulated, subtract one point. This sequence should also be treated as if it contained an error. If an error occurs in the following sequence, testing in that modality would be finished.
3. When it is obvious that a child has made an error in the middle of a sequence, score that sequence from the beginning to the middle and from the end to the middle. We suggest this practice because it has been found in memory research that errors are most probable in the middle of a sequence. Conversely, correct responses are more likely to occur at the beginning and end of a sequence. Scoring from the beginning and end toward the center will favor the child slightly without artificially inflating the score.
4. As a general rule, look for correct rather than incorrect responses. There are many reasons for a child to do more poorly on an instrument than he or she is able, but few circumstances that increase a child's score. Marking as correct those responses that are uncertain results in a total score that is a better indication of the child's true ability than does a scoring system that is negatively biased.
5. Above all, be consistent. Not all scoring possibilities can be anticipated, so common sense and consistency are perhaps the best scoring guidelines we can recommend.

When the administration of the test is completed, all correct responses should be marked on the record sheet. Tabulate the number of correct responses in each modality; this is the raw score for that modality. The three modality raw scores, when added together, equal the total raw score.

To identify the relative strength of each modality, it is necessary to compute the percentage of the total score each modality represents. This can be done by dividing the raw score for each modality by the total raw score. The following example typifies this process.

A child's modality raw scores are as follows: Visual, 19; Auditory, 13; Kinesthetic, 9. The sum of these values is 41; this is the total raw score. The percentage scores for each modality are:

$$\frac{\text{Visual raw score}}{\text{Total raw score}} = \frac{19}{41} = 46.3\%$$

$$\frac{\text{Auditory raw score}}{\text{Total raw score}} = \frac{13}{41} = 31.7\%$$

$$\frac{\text{Kinesthetic raw score}}{\text{Total raw score}} = \frac{9}{41} = 22.0\%$$

A complete table for converting raw scores into percentages can be found in Appendix A.

## Interpretation of Modality Percentage Scores

The interpretation of modality percentage scores is based on our observation that a difference of about five points corresponds to an educationally relevant difference. What this means is that if the percentage score in one modality is at least five points greater than that of another modality, the first modality is the stronger of the two. If one modality is five percentage points greater than each of the remaining modalities, it is the dominant modality.

In the example we have presented, vision would be the dominant modality, since the visual percentage is five points greater than the auditory percentage and the kinesthetic percentage. In addition, the auditory modality appears superior to the kinesthetic modality. The child with a profile of modality percentage scores similar to that in the example would have a dominant visual modality and a secondary auditory modality. Teaching this child would be most effective if material were presented visually. Supplemental material could be presented auditorily if for some reason the lesson were not amenable to visual display or additional practice in another modality were needed.

*Observing the child during the administration of the SBMI.* One of the important aspects of the SBMI is teacher observation. Frequently, children's behavior while studying and reproducing a pattern will provide clues to their preferred modality. Learn to watch each child during the administration of the SBMI and take note of his or her behaviors. Children who are visual may close their eyes, or look off into space or at a blank wall in order to help them concentrate and remember the visual images. By doing this, they are blocking out visual distractions. Kinesthetic children may use their hands in some way to help them remember the number of shapes in a sequence or to somehow form the shapes as they see or hear them. Auditory children tend to say the names of the shapes to themselves. You may see them move their lips or they may even say the shapes aloud.

Notice at the end of each modality subtest that there is a question to ask the child and a place on the record sheet to write the answer. The child may say that he or she said the names of the shapes, or tried to remember what the shapes looked like, or drew imaginary lines to represent the shapes.

When interpreting your observations and the child's remarks, be careful not to be misled by first impressions. A child's behaviors in the beginning may not indicate his or her true modality strength. For example, many children will say the names of the shapes to themselves during the testing. Not all of these children are auditory. Watch for other, more significant behaviors in children, behaviors that would indicate a visual or kinesthetic preference. At first, an individual may use every way he or she knows to remember a sequence. But as the sets get longer and more difficult, the person will rely on one modality in order to remember.

The following illustrations will explain further the interpretation of the results of the SBMI. Table 1 presents the percentage profiles of three children, Jean, George, and Charles. All three are approximately the same age and are in the same grade. Using the five percentage point criterion we recommend, Jean would be termed primarily kinesthetic, George would have a dominant auditory modality and a secondary visual modality, and Charles would have mixed modality strengths.

Jean's strongest modality is obviously the kinesthetic. The difference

**Table 1 MODALITY PERCENTAGE SCORES FOR THREE CHILDREN**

|            | Jean | George | Charles |
|------------|------|--------|---------|
| Visual     | 28   | 39     | 35      |
| Auditory   | 31   | 53     | 31      |
| Kinesthetic| 41   | 8      | 34      |

between the Visual and Auditory Subtests is only three percentage points, and is not great enough to be educationally noteworthy. It is important to note, however, that on both the Visual and Auditory Subtests, Jean used her fingers to hold spaces and keep track of the number of shapes in the sequences. Jean involves motor activity in learning.

George's dominant modality is the auditory, but the difference between his Kinesthetic and Visual Subtests is much more than five percentage points. His secondary modality is therefore vision. In teaching George, it would be most logical to rely first on auditory cues, and then on visual cues. Providing kinesthetic experiences for George will be of little help.

During the Kinesthetic Subtest, George repeatedly expressed his desire to stop the test. He vocalized the names of the shapes in the sequences and asked the examiner to confirm a shape name (which the examiner did not do). The low score on George's Kinesthetic Subtest and his dissatisfaction with the testing method imply that kinesthetic activities might interfere with his learning.

Charles evidenced no dominant modality; his percentage scores were fairly consistent, so he can be said to have mixed modality strengths. He is likely to benefit from material presented in any modality, and could profitably be exposed to multisensory materials.

From the discussion thus far, it is obvious that interpreting the SBMI depends on the interaction of the actual numerical scores obtained and the observations of the tester. If numbers are all that are desired, numbers can be obtained from the Swassing-Barbe Modality Index. However, the SBMI should be considered more than a device for obtaining percentages. It is a systematic series of tasks designed to provide a standard means of making judgments about the modality strengths of the person taking the test. Consequently, observing the child in the testing setting is an important source of information. This information should be used to temper any interpretations of the numerical scores that result from the SBMI.

You may have noticed that no comparisons were made among the performances of Jean, George, and Charles. No one performance was better or worse than another performance. The important difference is in how the percentage scores were distributed. It is this difference that is educationally important and defines individual differences. Each of the three performances was correct—appropriate for each of the three youngsters.

## Observable Characteristics Indicative of Modality Strength

An individual's ability to identify modality strength simply through observation can be expected to become increasingly more accurate. Information about the modalities and practice in identifying modality strengths sensitize an individual to the point that testing sometimes becomes unnecessary. In fact, for a skilled observer, the use of the SBMI is recommended only in those cases where verification of observation is needed, or when there are conflicting and therefore confusing behaviors.

The list of characteristics included in this chapter is intended to serve as a guide for the individual who wishes to become more sensitive to modality related behaviors of children. It is not meant to establish hard and fast rules, or even to suggest that such behaviors always indicate one specific modality strength. The sources of the characteristics were the comments of teachers and parents and the observations of the authors. These observations have not yet been verified through research activities, but we are confident that such verification will ensue.

Care must be taken to avoid labeling a child on the basis of one or two isolated behaviors. The most reliable observations, of course, are those that have been made over an extensive time period and in a variety of situations. It is also important to keep in mind that no individual relies exclusively on only one modality. Every individual, unless there is a physical disability, makes use of all the educationally relevant modalities. Therefore, a person may at various times behave in a way that might indicate any one of the three major modalities.

The characteristics summarized in Table 2 are a good basis for observing a child's behavior. The reader may wish to add to the table, or construct a table based on personal observations. We encourage this practice, with one caution: avoid projecting one's own modality strength into the list. It is easy to see the world through our own eyes, but such a perspective is too limited to be of general use. To be sure that characteristics have general application, try them out on another person. Feedback of this kind can be of great assistance in a personal list of modality related behaviors.

### Table 2 OBSERVABLE CHARACTERISTICS INDICATIVE OF MODALITY STRENGTH

| | Visual | Auditory | Kinesthetic |
|---|---|---|---|
| Learning Style | Learns by seeing; watching demonstrations | Learns through verbal instructions from others or self | Learns by doing; direct involvement |
| Reading | Likes description; sometimes stops reading to stare into space and imagine scene; intense concentration | Enjoys dialogue, plays; avoids lengthy description, unaware of illustrations; moves lips or subvocalizes | Prefers stories where action occurs early; fidgets when reading, handles books; not an avid reader |
| Spelling | Recognizes words by sight; relies on configuration of words | Uses a phonics approach; has auditory word attack skills | Often is a poor speller; writes words to determine if they "feel" right |
| Handwriting | Tends to be good, particularly when young; spacing and size are good; appearance is important | Has more difficulty learning in initial stages; tends to write lightly; says strokes when writing | Good initially, deteriorates when space becomes smaller; pushes harder on writing instrument |
| Memory | Remembers faces, forgets names; writes things down, takes notes | Remembers names, forgets faces; remembers by auditory repetition | Remembers best what was done, not what was seen or talked about |
| Imagery | Vivid imagination; thinks in pictures, visualizes in detail | Subvocalizes, thinks in sounds; details less important | Imagery not important; images that do occur are accompanied by movement |
| Distractibility | Generally unaware of sounds; distracted by visual disorder or movement | Easily distracted by sounds | Not attentive to visual, auditory presentation so seems distractible |
| Problem Solving | Deliberate; plans in advance; organizes thoughts by writing them; lists problems | Talks problems out, tries solutions verbally, subvocally; talks self through problem | Attacks problems physically; impulsive; often selects solution involving greatest activity |

## Table 2   (continued)

|  | Visual | Auditory | Kinesthetic |
|---|---|---|---|
| Response to Periods of Inactivity | Stares; doodles; finds something to watch | Hums; talks to self or to others | Fidgets; finds reasons to move; holds up hand |
| Response to New Situations | Looks around; examines structure | Talks about situation, pros and cons, what to do | Tries things out; touches, feels; manipulates |
| Emotionality | Somewhat repressed; stares when angry; cries easily, beams when happy; facial expression is a good index of emotion | Shouts with joy or anger; blows up verbally but soon calms down; expresses emotion verbally and through changes in tone, volume, pitch of voice | Jumps for joy; hugs, tugs, and pulls when happy; stamps, jumps, and pounds when angry, stomps off; general body tone is a good index of emotion |
| Communication | Quiet; does not talk at length; becomes impatient when extensive listening is required; may use words clumsily; describes without embellishment; uses words such as *see*, *look*, etc. | Enjoys listening but cannot wait to talk; descriptions are long but repetitive; likes hearing self and others talk; uses words such as *listen*, *hear*, etc. | Gestures when speaking; does not listen well; stands close when speaking or listening; quickly loses interest in detailed verbal discourse; uses words such as *get*, *take*, etc. |
| General Appearance | Neat, meticulous, likes order; may choose not to vary appearance | Matching clothes not so important, can explain choices of clothes | Neat but soon becomes wrinkled through activity |
| Response to the Arts | Not particularly responsive to music; prefers the visual arts; tends not to voice appreciation of art of any kind, but can be deeply affected by visual displays; focuses on details and components rather than the work as a whole | Favors music; finds less appeal in visual art, but is readily able to discuss it; misses significant detail, but appreciates the work as a whole; is able to develop verbal association for all art forms; spends more time talking about pieces than looking at them | Responds to music by physical movement; prefers sculpture; touches statues and paintings; at exhibits stops only at those in which he or she can become physically involved; comments very little on any art form |

## Summary

The earliest methods of identifying modality strengths were purely observational. These were supplemented by structured activities in the latter part of the nineteenth and early part of the twentieth centuries. It was not until 1961 that a test was developed to assess more than one modality; this was the Illinois Test of Psycholinguistic Abilities.

Since the development of the ITPA, other instruments have appeared that were intended to assess modality strengths. These instruments were either too time consuming, required too much training for appropriate administration, or measured preferences rather than strengths. The need for a practical tool that was usable by teachers to measure students' modality strengths prompted the development of the SBMI.

The SBMI is a valid and reliable instrument that determines modality strengths through a matching-to-sample task. The student is presented a model, a set of shapes in sequences of increasing length, and asked to reconstruct the model. The models are presented in each of the educationally relevant modalities. The student's performance on the SBMI is reported as percentage scores in each modality. This allows a student's relative modality strengths to be compared, but does not permit one student's performance to be compared to that of another's.

The SBMI is actually intended to complement teacher observations. In order to assist teachers in developing acute observation skills, the chapter includes a check list which summarizes behaviors frequently associated with a particular modality strength.

## References

Dechant, E.V. and Smith, H.P. *Psychology in teaching reading* (2nd ed.) Englewood Cliffs, NJ: Prentice-Hall, 1977.

Dunn, R.S. and Dunn, K.J. *Learning Style Inventory*. Lawrence, Kan.: Price Systems, 1975.

————. Learning styles/teaching styles: should they . . . can they . . . be matched? *Educational Leadership,* 1979, *36,* 238–244.

Kirk, S.A.; McCarthy, J.J.; and Kirk, W.D. *Illinois Test of Psycholinguistic Abilities (Experimental Edition)*. Urbana: University of Illinois, 1961.

————. *Illinois Test of Psycholinguistic Abilities*. Urbana: University of Illinois, 1968.

Mills, R.E. *The teaching of word recognition*. Ft. Lauderdale: The Mills School, 1970.

Montessori, M. *Dr. Montessori's own handbook*. New York: Schochen, 1914.

CHAPTER IV

# Standardization
# of the SBMI

This chapter describes the first large-scale application of the pilot version of the Swassing-Barbe Modality Index. The purposes of the research described herein were to determine the psychometric properties of the SBMI, and to examine the relationship between scores on the SBMI and selected personal characteristics of the sample of students to which it was administered.

The material presented in this chapter is in narrative form with only two figures. A more detailed description of the results of the standardization research, including extensive tables and figures, can be found in Appendix B. The primary consumers of the SBMI—teachers, school administrators, and other educational practitioners—should find the current presentation sufficient to justify their use of the instrument. They may also wish to refer to the more technically oriented presentation.

*The standardization sample.* A large southern California elementary school district agreed to test their students and provide the supplemental student information required. Over 600 students in grades kindergarten through six completed the test. As would be expected for this age range, boys in the sample slightly outnumbered girls, and there were approximately nine right-handed children for each left-handed child.

These proportions are consistent with the national figures for sex and handedness. With respect to race, however, the standardization sample was atypical. A disproportionately large number of students, about 30 percent of the sample, were of Hispanic origin. The proportion of white to black students in the sample approximated the national ratio.

There was some concern that the large number of Hispanic students would bias the results. Fortunately, no discrepancy in the scores of these students emerged. We are confident that our findings can be generalized to the majority of elementary school students throughout the country.

*Procedures.* One of the developers of the SBMI visited the school district that provided the subjects. He tested over fifty reading specialists himself, trained them in the use of the SBMI, and provided them with pre-publication versions of the instrument. These reading specialists, in turn, tested all of the children available in the district.

Completed scoring sheets and selected personal characteristics of the children who composed the sample were returned to the researchers. These data were entered into a computer and analyzed using a statistical package that performs routine data analyses.

## Psychometric Properties of the SBMI

Before any measurement tool can be used by educational practitioners, it must be demonstrated that the tool is both valid and reliable. Validity refers to the degree to which an instrument measures what it is supposed to measure, while reliability describes the consistency or stability of the results obtained by the instrument.

An example is presented here to clarify the concepts of validity and reliability. Stepping on your bathroom scale in the morning, you would be surprised if, instead of your weight, your blood pressure appeared. You might also be suspicious, since the equipment necessary to measure blood pressure is not found in bathroom scales. It is doubtful that you would give much credence to the scale as an index of blood pressure. In other words, the scale would not be a valid measure of blood pressure.

Now, suppose you weighed yourself on the scale and found that you weighed 130 pounds. Later the same day, while undergoing a routine physical examination, your physician's scale also indicated that you weighed 130 pounds. You would be confident that your bathroom scale was valid, and was not registering a weight that reflected the unevenness of the floor or the amount of force you applied when stepping on the scale.

The same example can be extended to reliability. Upon seeing that you weighed only 130 pounds, you immediately informed your spouse that you had lost ten pounds. Your spouse was somewhat skeptical, so both of you returned to the bathroom, where you weighed yourself again. The scale registered 130 pounds, and your spouse's skepticism vanished. You demonstrated that your scale is reliable, since it registered the same weight consistently.

*Validity.* There are several types of validity, one of which is face or logical validity. Face validity is not computed through a statistical test, but is determined solely on the basis of common sense standards. Using such standards, it seems that the tasks that constitute the SBMI are a function of the modalities the test is intended to measure. There is little question that the stimuli presented in each of the modality subtests are appropriate stimuli for that modality. The SBMI, therefore, can be described as having high face validity.

Face validity is held in no great esteem by test developers, since no statistic is associated with it. Test users, however, place great store in face validity, and feel more confident using an instrument that appeals to their logic. An instrument may possess high statistical validity, but if it does not inspire the confidence of the users, it will remain unused.

Another type of validity is criterion validity. This refers to the degree to which an instrument is associated with an acknowledged measure of the characteristic in question. As yet, no tests of the criterion validity of the SBMI have been conducted, for there is no criterion that is a widely accepted measure of the modality strengths which we are describing. There are several instruments that may provide appropriate criteria, and plans are underway to compare the SBMI to these instruments.

Construct validity is a measure of the conformity between the structure of a test as hypothesized by its developers and the actual performance of subjects on the test. If, for example, you were to develop a test of basketball ability, you would expect professional basketball players to perform better on the test than elementary school students.

One way of measuring construct validity is through factor analysis. This procedure is simply a statistical method of sorting items according to common characteristics. A factor analysis identifies the items or subtests on which subjects perform similarly. With respect to the SBMI, it was believed that the three modality subtests would emerge as clear and unrelated factors. If they did, then we could be relatively sure that we were measuring three separate skills.

The factor analysis conducted on modality raw scores produced very encouraging results. Three factors emerged, corresponding to the visual, kinesthetic, and auditory modalities. In addition, we found that we were measuring another characteristic, one that was related to each of the modalities. This other characteristic appears to be short term memory. Thus, in addition to verifying that we were measuring three separate modalities, the factor analysis supported our contention that memory is a constituent of what we are calling modality.

The final type of validity that we will touch upon is indirect validity, which shows what a test does not measure. Indirect validity is of great importance when the test being developed has the potential to measure a trait that is related to the target characteristic, but is not the target characteristic itself.

The most obvious characteristic other than modality strength that the SBMI could be tapping is achievement. To determine whether or not this was actually the case, we conducted a factor analysis that included both modality scores and achievement as measured by the Comprehensive Tests of Basic Skills (McGraw-Hill, 1975). The first factor that resulted was clearly achievement, while the second comprised the modality variables. Since achievement and modality scores loaded on separate and unrelated factors we contend that the SBMI is not measuring achievement.

*Reliability*. The most commonly used means of determining the reliability of an instrument are stability and internal consistency. Stability, also known as test-retest reliability, tells us if subjects' scores change predictably from one time to another. When the SBMI was administered to a group of students twice over a span of approximately four months, it proved to be at least as stable as other measures of modality strength. The test-retest reliability of the subtests of the SBMI ranged from .58 to .67, falling within the acceptable limits for an instrument of this type.

The structure of the SBMI prevents the use of traditional measures of internal consistency. The subtests of the SBMI do, however, resemble a type of scale often used in the social sciences, a Guttman scale. This scale is an index or measure that is unidimensional and cumulative. That is, the items that constitute a Guttman scale must all measure the same underlying dimension, and they must be ordered by the degree of difficulty.

Although a Guttman scale does not provide a measure of internal consistency, it is associated with statistics that can be interpreted in much the same way as are measures of internal consistency. One of these is a coefficient of reproducibility, which indicates how well an individual's response pattern can be predicted from the individual's score on the most difficult item completed. On a perfect Guttman scale, if an individual answered item five correctly, but not item six, you would expect the individual to have responded to items one through four correctly and items seven through nine incorrectly.

The coefficients of reproducibility for the subtests of the SBMI are all above .90, suggesting that the instrument conforms to the structure of an acceptable Guttman scale. Further, the coefficients of scalability for the subtests approach or exceed .60. The latter measure is an indication of the consistency of the scale. A good ruler, for instance, will have its inch indicators spaced evenly; a poor ruler will be characterized by slightly inconsistent spacing between inch marks. With coefficients of scalability in the region of .60, the user can be confident that the instrument is measuring with comparative consistency.

## The Relationship Between Modality Strengths and Sex, Handedness, and Grade

As is the case with many other psychoeducational assessment tools, students' performance on the SBMI varies as a function of certain personal characteristics. This portion of the chapter will discuss variations in performance that appear to be related to sex, handedness, and grade. Grade rather than age was selected because our research suggests that the educational experience itself is as important an influence on modality strength as is maturation. Grade placement is a better measure of the combined influences of schooling and maturation than is age alone.

When the modality scores of boys and girls were compared within each grade, no statistically significant differences emerged. This finding is consistent with the contention of Maccoby and Jacklin (1974) that the perceptual skills of elementary school age boys and girls are similar. We would like to add, however, that the girls' raw scores on the SBMI were consistently higher than the boys' raw scores. Further, the Maccoby and Jacklin contention referred to perceptual skills that did not correspond perfectly with the definition of modality we are supporting. Therefore, it is possible that the female advantage we have noted represents an actual difference in modality functioning during the elementary school years.

Left-handed and right-handed children in our sample showed no differences in their modality raw scores or percentages. This suggests that modality strengths are not related to hemispheric dominance and that the opportunity to practice within each modality is the same for right and left-handed children.

Since sex and handedness appear to exert very little influence on modality performance, it is appropriate to consider modality raw scores and percentages only as a function of grade. The changes in modality scores as a function of grade, represented in Figures 1 and 2, are quite striking.

From Figure 1, it can be seen that modality raw scores increase monotonically as a function of grade. In other words, the ability to function in each modality increases steadily during the elementary school years. This increase reflects the cognitive development that is taking place between the ages of five and twelve.

Modality percentage scores change in a much less consistent manner. There is more variability between grades, and the trend is more subtle. A close look at Figure 2, however, suggests that the relative strength of the visual and kinesthetic modalities increases between grades kindergarten and six, while the relative importance of audition is decreasing. This contention can be confirmed by referring to the raw scores depicted in Figure 1. Auditory raw scores increase during the elementary school years, but at a much slower rate than either visual or kinesthetic raw scores.

The differential rate of change among the modality scores is important, because it suggests that the educational process itself has an influence on modality strengths. During the preschool years, children interact with their peers and adults primarily through oral/aural means. The result is extensive opportunity to practice in the auditory modality and great reliance upon this channel. During elementary school, however, audition is supplanted by vision and kinesthesia as reading and writing occupy a significant role in the child's life. Audition, although it remains one of the major modalities, plays a less prominent role than it did before the child entered school.

As the child matures, another phenomenon occurs: the modalities become more integrated. The differences among modality percentage scores decrease with age, suggesting that one of the concomitants of maturation is that strategies are developed to transfer information from one modality to another. This conclusion is well supported by child development research (Chalfant and Scheffelin, 1969).

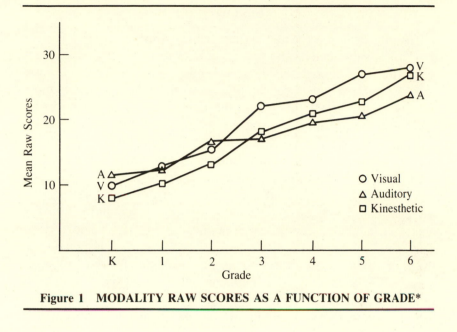

**Figure 1    MODALITY RAW SCORES AS A FUNCTION OF GRADE***

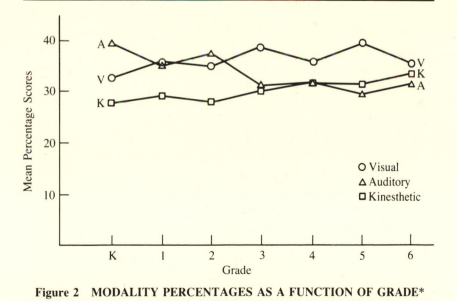

**Figure 2    MODALITY PERCENTAGES AS A FUNCTION OF GRADE***

*Tabular summaries of the data corresponding to these figures can be found in Appendix B, Supplemental Tables 18 and 19.

## Summary

The information presented argues that the SBMI is a measurement tool that is sufficiently valid and reliable to merit use by educational professionals. Although the criterion validity of the instrument has not yet been proven, the face validity, construct validity, and indirect validity of the SBMI fall within the acceptable range. In terms of reliability, the instrument is stable over time and possesses the characteristics of a satisfactory Guttman scale.

Sex and handedness have little influence on modality strengths when grade is taken into consideration. With respect to grade, modality raw scores increase monotonically between kindergarten and sixth grade. As reflected by both percentage and raw scores, the auditory modality decreases in relative importance through the elementary school grades. This may be attributed to the amount of practice in each modality in the preschool and elementary school years. Audition is most frequently used before the child enters school; during the school years, as a result of learning to read and write, vision and kinesthesia enjoy greater use. The result is that vision and kinesthesia take precedence over audition by the time the child reaches sixth grade.

## References

Chalfant, J.C. and Scheffelin, M.A. *Central processing dysfunctions in children: a review of research.* U.S. Department of Health, Education, and Welfare, National Institute of Neurological Diseases and Stroke, 1969.

Maccoby, E.E. and Jacklin, C.N. *The psychology of sex differences.* Palo Alto, Calif.: Stanford University Press, 1974.

McGraw-Hill. *Comprehensive Test of Basic Skills.* 1975.

# CHAPTER V

# The Practice of Modality-Based Instruction

Previous chapters have focused upon the concepts underlying modality-based instruction, its history, and the assessment of modality strengths. Now we come to what is perhaps the most crucial chapter in the text, the practice of modality-based instruction. The importance of this chapter rests on our belief that the application of an instructional method in the classroom is the only true test of its worth.

## What Is Modality-Based Instruction?

Modality-based instruction is a comprehensive approach to education with the central tenet that instruction is organized around a student's learning strength. It includes a wide variety of components and has applications at all levels of instruction. Preschool teachers will find it helpful to rely upon the modality strengths of their students, as will teachers in high school, college, and adult education. Elementary education has served as the focus of this text, but there is no need to think that the principles we are outlining are limited to young children.

The techniques and materials that constitute modality-based instruction can be grouped under two headings:

*Initial teaching strategies.* Modifications are made to initial teaching strategies based upon an awareness that both teachers and students have modality strengths. Such modifications are comparatively minor, and often involve simply an understanding on the part of the teacher that a lesson in which the class is involved will be grasped more readily by one type of learner than another.

*The point of intervention.* Strategies under this heading are used if the teacher discovers that after presenting the material initially, a student or group of students has failed to grasp the content of the lesson. At this point, called the *point of intervention,* the teacher presents the material again, not in the same mode, but this time in the mode that is strongest for a particular student.

Modality-based instruction can be applied at all levels of schooling, and has value in both initial teaching and in remediation. But, is it different from other methods in any fundamental way? We think it is. An example based on Bloom's (1956) *Taxonomy of Educational Objectives* will illustrate this point.

Knowing a concept, fact, or rule is a preliminary step toward applying it. Therefore, most approaches to education focus initially on knowledge. Unfortunately, if the initial goal (knowledge) is antithetical to a child's learning strength, accomplishing the ultimate goal (application) may be prolonged unnecessarily. A shortcoming inherent in any unimodal approach is that initial objectives are antithetical to the learning strengths of the majority of children in the classroom.

Take, for instance, the use of phonics to teach reading to a visual learner. For this child, the initial goal, knowledge of the sounds associated with certain letters or combinations of letters, may be unnecessary. In fact, focusing on this initial objective may hinder the accomplishment of the ultimate objective, reading. The visual learner will have difficulty with phonics, but can master it with effort. Recognizing words on sight is much more easily accomplished. By-passing the initial goal of the phonics approach will result in a more rapid accomplishment of the ultimate goal.

We are not suggesting that modality-based instruction ignore initial learning objectives. These beginning steps play just as an important a role in modality-based instruction as they do in other approaches. What we are implying is that modality-based instruction helps the teacher select more appropriate initial objectives, resulting in more direct advancement of the ultimate goal, application of the skill.

**What modality-based instruction is not.** Any discussion of modality-based instruction would be incomplete if it failed to examine what the approach does not entail. As with any new concept, or the application of any concept in a different manner, there are bound to be some areas in which there is disagreement, or at best, only partial agreement. This should not be viewed negatively, for as our knowledge of modality-based instruction increases, more applications can be expected. To avoid misunderstanding though, some clarification is in order. This section delineates those practices which are not part of modality-based instruction.

*Modality-based instruction is not deficit-oriented.* The emphasis of modality-based instruction is not on weaknesses, but on strengths.

From what the child has already learned, the teacher has a clue as to what and how the child can learn. Instead of the prevailing approach, which attempts to identify what the child does not know and then prescribe ways of overcoming his or her deficiency, modality-based instruction attempts to devise ways of presenting the same material through the child's area of strength.

*Modality-based instruction is not multisensory instruction.* Multisensory instruction generally takes two forms, either a "shotgun" or a "cafeteria." In the "shotgun" approach, a barrage of multisensory information is directed toward a class in the hope that every student's learning strength will be hit by at least part of the lesson. Some publishers are promoting multisensory materials primarily because it is a safe approach. Safe, yes, but it is not universally effective. Students with mixed modalities may benefit from the "shotgun" approach, as may those students with single modality strengths and highly developed attending skills. For some students, however, multisensory presentations of this kind are counterproductive. Information offered simultaneously in the major modalities will be distracting at best, and at worst will actually inhibit learning. Modality-based instruction, as we see it, is not a "shotgun" approach.

Neither is modality-based instruction a "cafeteria" approach to education, in which a lesson is taught through a single modality, then the lesson is repeated in another modality and finally, the same material is presented through the remaining modality. The "cafeteria" approach, in theory, has a certain appeal. Is not the lesson tailored to fit the modality strengths of each student? The problem is that most of the class is ignored for two-thirds of the lesson. In practice, it is little different from "round robin" reading in which each child must patiently wait for a turn to read. The kinesthetic learner, in particular, suffers. Auditory learners can tune out irrelevant aspects of the lesson, and visual learners will stare out the window. The kinesthetic learner, however, may fidget, hit the child in the next seat, drop books, and end up in the principal's office.

Another limitation of the "cafeteria" approach is that, like the "shotgun" approach, it can inhibit learning. Material that is currently being presented may interfere with the retention of previous material (retroactive inhibition) or the acquisition of new material (proactive inhibition). When this occurs, learning is suppressed and the child may lose confidence in his or her ability to function in school.

*Modality-based instruction does not require that children with similar modalities be grouped.* Initial teaching in modality-based instruction should be done with the entire class. Individualizing or personalizing instruction follows initial instruction, and when several students with the same modality strengths need additional instruction, grouping is a logical procedure.

Caution must be observed during initial instruction to avoid labeling children by modality strength and then limiting instruction to this area only. Ultimately, it is advantageous to learn to use all of one's senses. Initially grouping children of the same modality may result in better immediate learning, but will have the long term consequence of restricting a child's potential by delaying the integration of the modalities.

*Modality-based instruction does not require that the teacher have the same modality as the student being taught.* It is imperative that the teacher understand modality, be aware of the modality strength of the student, and be aware of her or his own modality strength in order to avoid the unconscious adapting of instruction into her or his own mode. If these conditions are met, there is no reason to suspect that the teacher, regardless of modality strength, cannot adapt instruction into each of the three major modes of instruction.

## Initial Teaching Strategies

The most important initial teaching strategy is perhaps not a strategy at all, but a frame of mind. A teacher who is aware that modality strengths influence the selection of instructional activities, and who realizes that the same lesson will be received differently by students with differing modality strengths, is likely to be a more effective teacher. The following will illustrate this.

*A visit to a classroom.* Ms. Cullen, a third grade teacher, is in the middle of a spelling lesson. Her strength is in the visual mode and she uses a visual method of teaching spelling. She is aware, however, that her modality strength is not shared by every student in the class, and has adapted her lesson somewhat to accommodate the variety of modality strengths exhibited by her students. During the lesson, we slip through the back door of the classroom.

The first student to notice our arrival is Kit, an auditory learner. Even though we tried to slip into the room quietly, Kit turned in her chair to find out who had come into the class.

The teacher is standing at the chalkboard pointing at each letter of the word written on the board. She addresses the class, "This is our first word. Look how it starts with a maximum letter, has two minimum letters in the middle, and ends with an intermediate letter."

Kit, in the meantime, has picked up her pencil and taps her desk each time Ms. Cullen points to a letter. As the teacher points to the letters that constitute the word, Kit is sounding them out to herself "el, o, u, duh."

Ms. Cullen draws a line around the word to accentuate its configuration. Kit winces when the chalk makes a screeching sound as it is drawn across the board. While the teacher discusses the shape of the word, Kit is continuing to repeat to herself the sequence of sounds in the word. She is listening to herself, not the teacher, as she puts the sounds together to form the word *loud*.

*"Loud,"* she says to herself. "It means very noisy. I like to make all kinds of sounds. I guess I must be loud. But we're supposed to be quiet in class, except when we get to read aloud. Loud!"

While these thoughts are going through Kit's mind, the teacher has finished describing the configuration of the word. She turns to the class and says, "Who knows what this word means? How about you, Kit, you're a good speller. Tell us what letters are in this word and what it means."

Kit hesitates for a moment while looking at the word on the board. She is confirming that she has all the sounds right. Then she says confidently, *"l, o, u, d. Loud.* It means noisy."

The teacher smiles and replies, "That's right, Kit. You are such a good speller." Ms. Cullen knows that Kit is an auditory learner, and does not insist that she use the configuration cues. Ms. Cullen also realizes that the hesitation Kit showed before she spoke was not a sign that she did not know the answer, but indicated that Kit was transferring the letters from the visual display on the board to a series of sounds that she said to herself. Not only can Kit learn through the auditory modality, she can transfer cues from other modalities into the auditory.

As the teacher begins the next word in the lesson, we shift our attention to Hanley. During our visit, aside from a glance around the room, she has remained very still. Her eyes are glued to the chalkboard.

"Our second word is different from the first. It starts with a maximum letter, then has four minimum letters. The word is *brown,* and it is a color." Hanley looks at the letters *b, r, o, w, n.* She closes her eyes for a moment, opens them, and looks at the word again. She takes her pencil and writes the word on her paper. "No," she says to herself, "that doesn't look right. I know the first letter is right, and the last letter is *n,* I know that's right." She looks up at the chalkboard again. "Oh, that's a *w,* not a *u.* Those letters look alike. *W,* wood is brown and starts with *w* and *brown* has a *w* in it." Hanley crosses out her misspelled word and writes the word correctly this time. "That's it."

"Hanley, what is the word?"

*"Brown."*

"Can you spell *brown?"*

*"B, r, o, w, n. Brown."*

"Good work, Hanley. See how easy it is if you just look at the word. Look at it carefully, and get a good picture of it in your mind."

Ms. Cullen points to the third word on the list and begins to discuss the shape of the word. During the entire lesson, Cy, a kinesthetic learner, has been busy looking for his pencil—moving books around and rubbing his hands over a pile of paper to see if he could feel it. He pushes his feet around under the desk to see if he can kick the pencil out into plain sight. As he becomes aware that attention is on him, his workbook falls to the floor.

Cy knows he was not paying attention. Ms. Cullen sees this, and says, "Why don't you come up to the board, Cy. Take this chalk and trace over the letters that make up this word." Cy walks to the front of the room and takes the chalk from Ms. Cullen.

The word on the board is *contest.* Cy begins tracing the letters while Ms. Cullen describes the word. Cy manages to trace over the word four times by the time Ms. Cullen has described it to the class. The teacher tells the class what the word is, and asks if anyone knows what it means. Before any of the other children can answer, Cy says, "It's like a race. You try to win against other people. Yesterday, Charles and I had a contest to see who could swing the highest." Cy has walked over to Charles' desk and is standing beside it. It almost seems as if Cy is ready to start the contest again.

"Very good, Cy. I know you like contests. Why don't you go back to your seat and write the word." The child returns to his seat, picks up his pencil, and begins to write the word. At first, his letters are very large, almost the same size they were on the chalkboard. Cy has simply used the same muscle movements he did at the board. Ms. Cullen notices this, and asks him to make his word smaller. Cy does this, eventually writing the word between the right lines. He walks up to Ms. Cullen to show her his work. She compliments him, and sends him back to his seat. She turns to us and says, "Cy sometimes spends more time in the aisles than in his chair."

Three children, three ways of learning. Kit knew how to spell the words because she could transfer the teacher's visual clues into her auditory strength by repeating the letters and sounds to herself. Hanley easily learned the spelling words because the lesson was taught through her own modality strength. Cy would have missed the lesson completely had the teacher presented the words only through visual or auditory means, since Cy does not yet know how to transfer auditory and visual cues into his kinesthetic strength. Ms. Cullen knows this, and by calling Cy to the board and allowing him to trace the letters, she is presenting the lesson to the boy in a way he can understand.

The adaptations to the lesson Ms. Cullen made were not difficult. They were based on her understanding of modality and her experience. She did not attempt to ignore her own preferred way of learning, nor did she force her method on her students. She began the lesson in the manner in which she was most confident and comfortable, and adapted it as she went along. By any criteria, Ms. Cullen is a good teacher.

In addition to being able to adapt her lessons to accommodate the learning strengths of her students, Ms. Cullen is also aware of the advantage of reinforcing students through their modality strengths. When Hanley, the visual learner, successfully completes an activity in her workbook, Ms. Cullen marks her paper with a favorable comment, pastes a star on the page, or provides some other visual sign of approval. For Kit, pasting a star on a page is not very effective, so Ms. Cullen is sure to spend a moment with her to tell her what a good job she did. Touching Cy on the shoulder or patting him on the back is the best immediate reinforcement Ms. Cullen has found for him.

Each day, toward the end of the afternoon, Ms. Cullen has a period during which students use the learning stations. Naturally, Cy favors the most active station. He has been constructing a model city in which all the buildings are labeled. Cy enjoys the physical activity involved in assembling the buildings, and is learning the names of each of them.

Hanley spends her free time with a stamp collection. The collection has become very extensive, since Ms. Cullen has been maintaining it for several years. Through the collection, Hanley has learned the names of many foreign countries and where they are located on the globe.

One learning station has a tape recorder and a headset. Kit prefers this station, and her favorite tape contains the sounds of familiar objects and everyday activities. Kit has begun cataloging the sounds by the name of the object or activity; later, she will match these names with pictures of the object or activity.

## The Point of Intervention

When should the teacher alter his or her teaching strategies to accommodate learning styles? The point of intervention occurs when the material has been initially presented by the teacher and one or more of the students in the class fail to grasp the material. Someone in the class is just not "getting it." The teacher should interpret the problem as if the child were saying, "I don't understand the way you have just taught the lesson. Now can you teach it in a way that I will understand?" Most often, teachers repeat what they have just done, only slower and louder, as if reduced rate and more volume will produce the desired outcome.

What the teacher should do is say, "Wait a minute, I know the child's modality is kinesthetic and I know mine is auditory. I have probably told the child what to do. If the child is going to understand, I will have to get the child physically involved." This is the point of intervention. Regular instruction has failed to produce learning on the child's part, and additional activities are necessary.

The point of intervention for children or adults in remedial classes, learning disability classes, or special education is when the material is first presented, for it must be assumed that the individual has already been exposed to initial teaching procedures and has failed to learn at this level. The very fact that the individual has been identified as being other than a regular learner necessitates special procedures, and means that teaching to the individual's modality strength must occur immediately. There is no longer time, nor any justifiable reason, to continue with an approach that has already proven futile.

At the point of intervention, there are two ways of changing the mode of instruction: grouping students, and directing students to materials on which they can work alone. Grouping students is the most efficient means of intervening, but can be undertaken only when several students with the same modality strength have failed to grasp a lesson. When this occurs, set aside a time when the remainder of the class is engaged in seatwork or is otherwise occupied. Work with those who did not understand the lesson the first time, but present it to them in the modality they favor.

The spelling lesson described previously in this chapter could be reiterated for kinesthetic learners by bringing them to the board to trace the letters of the words on which the lesson is focusing. Forget the general configuration of the words; they will not be looking at the word anyway. Concentrate on the movements necessary to trace the words. Have the students first write the words at the chalkboard, or assemble the words from letters made of wood or plastic. Follow this by allowing the students to work at their seats writing the words with crayons and pencils. Associate the words with some activity.

The list of possible activities that can be used with small groups at the point of intervention is endless. The most critical features of grouping by modality strengths at the point of intervention are:

1. Identifying the modality strengths of the students who failed to learn the lesson as it was initially presented.
2. Structuring the activities around the learning strengths of the children, not the teacher.
3. Making sure that the remainder of the class is occupied.

Grouping students who need additional work might be the most efficient tactic at the point of intervention, but the strategy that many teachers prefer is directing students to activities on which they can work alone. When students are given the opportunity to work at their own rate on materials that are geared to their modality strengths, it is likely that the students will reap the primary benefit intended—acquisition of a specific academic skill. In addition, the students will develop independence, self-confidence, and a more positive self-image. This secondary gain may actually prove to be more valuable than learning the target skill.

Before students can be directed to self-instructional materials, there are a number of conditions that must be met. Both the student and the teacher must clearly understand what is the intended outcome of the activity. It is then relatively easy to keep the child on task, and even easier to determine the effectiveness of the activity. Well-defined learning outcomes also diminish the likelihood that a student will feel that he or she is being punished.

Another condition is that the material to which the child is directed must truly be self-instructional and usable by the child. Nothing is more frustrating for teachers and students than having the student continually asking the teacher how to do this or that. The student does not relish the feeling of helplessness that comes from being unable to do something that the teacher insists is easy; and the teacher is inclined to reject a student who is engaged in what appears to be attention-getting behaviors. The use of ostensibly self-instructional materials that are not results in frustration for all parties involved.

There should be continuity between self-instructional materials and the lesson which prompted their use. Referring a child to an activity that is disjointed from the original lesson promotes a sense of separateness on the part of the child. The feeling is that, "I'm not good enough to do the lesson that everyone else is doing" instead of "this is the same lesson, just a different way of learning it." By ensuring continuity between materials and lessons the child remains part of the class, particularly if many of the children are at one time or another engaged in self-instructional activities.

## Modality-Based Instruction in Basic Skill Areas

The acquisition of fundamental skills is greatly dependent upon the learner receiving and retaining information in her or his strongest modality. These fundamental skills are taught in the early elementary school years, and it is at this time that children still rely primarily upon their dominant modality. For the most part, young school age children have not yet acquired the ability to integrate their modalities.

Integration of the modalities evolves spontaneously in some children. When these children encounter difficulty, they transfer the information from the modality of presentation to their strongest modality. For a large portion of the school population, however, this transfer is, at best, a haphazard process.

When the teacher's modality and the modality of the child match, learning will most likely occur because the teacher is prone to present information in the child's most efficient modality. Should the teacher's modality not match that of an individual student, either the teacher or the student must adapt. Ideally, either party should be able to make necessary adjustments. It is doubtful though that school children in the early grades can consciously adapt their learning styles, so the burden of responsibility at this level rests with the teacher. It is important, nevertheless, that students learn how to transfer information from other modalities to their strength. It is incumbent upon the teacher to promote the development of skills associated with transferring information from one modality to another.

## Modality-Based Instruction in Reading

The reading process, by its very nature, is primarily visual. The child must somehow be able to look at a word and understand it. If visual association were the only way to read, however, both auditory and kinesthetic learners would never be good readers. Fortunately, there are ways to teach reading that rely upon the kinesthetic and auditory modalities, as well as upon visual.

The kinesthetic learner has, in times past, encountered great difficulty in learning to read. Visual and auditory approaches to reading have predominated, and the kinesthetic learner has been left to his or her own devices. This need not be the case, for it is possible to teach reading kinesthetically if the teacher is attuned to this modality. Left-to-right and top-to-bottom progression, and the physical shapes of words, for example, can be taught through large and small muscle activities.

One of the characteristics of kinesthetic learners which has been viewed negatively in the past can be used as an aid to teaching reading. Finger pointing, a habit that teachers sought to extinguish, helps the kinesthetic child focus on the appropriate word in a sentence. During the initial stages of learning to read, finger pointing should be encouraged, not with one finger but with two. A young child will have less difficulty pointing with the index and second fingers simultaneously, and the width of these two fingers will serve to underline whole words rather than single letters.

It is important to recognize that kinesthetic learning can be fostered in two ways. The first and most direct way is actual physical involvement in an activity. When youngsters write on the chalkboard, count on their fingers, point with two fingers, or draw imaginary letters in the air, they are directly experiencing physical involvement. Many activities related to reading can be organized in this manner.

The second way of promoting kinesthetic learning is called upon when a direct experience is obviated. Under these circumstances, an indirect or vicarious experience can be planned. A vicarious experience is one in which the individual imagines participation in the event or activity. With respect to the kinesthetic modality, the child imagines participation in a physical activity by engaging in a parallel activity in the classroom. Vicarious activities greatly expand the opportunities for teaching through kinesthetic strength. A game like "Climb the Mountain" can be organized to let youngsters become vicariously involved in mountain climbing by correctly identifying words and moving "up the mountain." "Surfboard" is another game that can be played with words. The task is to ride the wave to the beach. Easy words represent small waves, and hard words are large waves. Missed words mean the youngster has fallen off the surfboard or "wiped out" and must find a new wave to ride. The first student to ride all the way to the beach or climb the mountain is the winner.

The easiest way to teach auditory learners to read is through word attack skills that rely on the sounds of letters. Further, since these learners prefer to say words as they read, they should be allowed or even taught to move their lips when reading.

Because phonics has been popular for the past several decades, it is likely that auditory children have learned to read more easily than they would have in years past when the "look-say" method was in vogue. It is also probable that auditory learners, even as adults, are sounding out words they read, even though they may not move their lips. This explains why some very good readers are slow readers: they subvocalize every word.

## Modality-Based Instruction in Handwriting

Handwriting is essentially a kinesthetic task, with some visual and no auditory components; many teachers feel that there is no way to teach writing effectively through modalities other than the kinesthetic. Quite the opposite is true. The following list of objectives can serve as the foundation of a handwriting curriculum that relies upon each of the three educationally relevant modalities (Barbe and Lucas, 1978).

1. Visual (with model)
   a. Given letter models, writes lower-case manuscript letters
   b. Given letter models, writes upper-case manuscript letters
   c. Given numeral models writes numerals *1–30*
   d. Given models, writes number words *one-ten*
   e. Given letter models, writes without reversal letters that are frequently reversed: *b-d, p-g-q*
   f. Given word models, writes without reversal words that are frequently reversed: *on-no, was-saw*

    g. Given letter models, writes lower-case letters grouped by similarity of strokes

    h. Given letter models, writes upper-case letters grouped by similarity of strokes

    i. Given models, writes punctuation marks: period, comma, question mark, exclamation mark, quotation marks

2. Auditory (with oral directions, letter name or strokes)

    a. Told letter names, writes lower-case manuscript letters

    b. Told letter names, writes upper-case manuscript letters

    c. Given letter sound, writes letter

    d. Told letter names, says letter strokes

    e. Told numeral names, writes numerals *1–30*

    f. Told number names, writes number words *one-ten*

    g. Given oral directions, writes lower-case letters grouped by similarity of strokes

    h. Given oral directions, writes upper-case letters grouped by similarity of strokes

    i. Told names of punctuation marks, writes: period, comma, question mark, exclamation mark, quotation marks

    j. Told letter names, writes without reversal letters that are frequently reversed: *b-d, p-g-q*

    k. Told words, writes without reversal words that are frequently reversed: *on-no, was-saw*

3. Kinesthetic (tracing, motioning, chalkboard)

    a. Given example, traces or motions in air lower-case letters grouped by similarity of strokes

    b. Given example, traces or motions in air upper-case letters grouped by similarity of strokes

    c. Given example, traces or motions numerals

## Modality-Based Instruction in Arithmetic

Arithmetic is the skill area in which modality-based teaching is most easily adapted. Because so much of arithmetic depends upon simple memorization, the teacher's main task is to devise modality specific strategies that promote memorization. Once the basic rules have been memorized, they are readily applied to more advanced mathematics.

In addition to memorization, arithmetic involves manipulation, such as adding two or more quantities. These manipulations are understood better when the child has the opportunity to perform them in his or her strongest modality.

There are more materials and methods available for teaching arithmetic to the kinesthetic learner than for any other subject. The abacus, Cuisinaire rods, and Chisanbop (Pearson, 1978) are three examples of tools that are useful for kinesthetic learners; there are countless others. In selecting appropriate materials there is really only one consideration to keep in mind: the kinesthetic learner comprehends initial arithmetic skills best when numbers are presented as concrete objects which can be handled and manipulated. With sufficient practice manipulating objects, and with normal cognitive development, the kinesthetic learner should be able to deal with numbers just as abstractly as does the visual or auditory learner.

Visual learners can acquire basic arithmetic skills without actual manipulations. Displays in workbooks or on the chalkboard are often all the visual learner requires. Until rules have been practiced enough to be memorized, visual learners often picture a problem in their mind and manipulate the components of the image in the same way the images appear on the chalkboard or in the workbook. When these displays are supplemented by visual exercises such as problems on flashcards, arithmetic skills are quickly learned.

Visual and kinesthetic learners require either direct or imagined manipulations as a prelude to rule acquisition. Auditory learners usually demonstrate the reverse learning progression. Through simple repetition, they can learn fundamental mathematics operations. After the rules have been acquired, they gain an understanding of what is taking place through actual or imagined manipulations. Many teachers have had the experience of drilling a student and being impressed with the student's knowledge of the multiplication tables, only to be disappointed when he or she could not demonstrate understanding by appropriately manipulating objects. This student was probably auditory, and would eventually be able to apply the rules, given enough practice with manipulations.

## Modality-Based Instruction in Spelling

If the child's dominant learning mode is visual, he or she will learn best by being given visual models of correctly spelled words. By pointing out the sequence of letters in the word, drawing shapes around the word to teach its configuration, and emphasizing visual similarities and differences between words, the child acquires an image of what the word looks like when it is spelled correctly. A visual learner often writes a new word and checks to see if it looks right.

For the child whose strongest learning mode is audition, the sounds of words will be the basis for teaching spelling. The phonics skills by which the auditory child learned reading can be generalized to spelling.

Listening to the correct pronunciation of a word, counting the syllables, listening for the sounds of the vowels, and auditorily identifying diphthongs and digraphs are all approaches for teaching the auditory child to spell.

The kinesthetic learner will learn to spell best by writing the word. Since the kinesthetic child seems to prefer using large muscles, it may be best to encourage writing the target words on the chalkboard or on unlined paper.

There is some belief that kinesthetic learners are helped by writing the word with different instruments. It helps them get a ''feel'' for the word. One very bright kinesthetic adult said that when she learned a new word she wrote it first with a pencil, then a pen, next with a crayon, and finally with a piece of chalk. Then when she wrote the word later, she could tell if it ''felt'' right.

It is probably wise to have kinesthetic learners assemble the word in spelling. Reaching for the letters, lifting them out of a box, and putting them together reinforces motor performance. This will reduce the interferences possible from writing a word. For kinesthetic children, the task of forming the letters correctly and trying to hear the word may be too great. Allowing them to assemble the words appears to work better when a reduction of interference is called for.

A brief discussion of spelling errors may help the reader understand why teaching spelling through modality strengths is such a potentially successful technique. As you might expect, auditory learners are inclined to say the words as they spell them, so they tend to make mistakes that relate to the sounds of words. Their words frequently contain enough syllables, but are not long enough. The auditory learner may confuse letters of different sizes, such as an intermediate letter with a maximum letter.

Visual learners almost always get the correct number of letters in words, and the initial and final letters will frequently be correct. The letters in the middle are more likely to be jumbled. Visual learners interchange minimum letters such as *e, o,* and *a,* but never confuse them with an intermediate letter like *t,* or with a tall letter like *l.* When marking the spelling papers of visual learners, teachers should not mark the incorrect words, for this will only reinforce the incorrect spelling. Rather, the teacher should write the words correctly and let the visual learners see the words spelled correctly. The first time the children are aware that they have misspelled a word, they see the correct model of the word.

Kinesthetic learners, for some reason, seem to be prone to auditory interference. One student said that when the teacher used a word in a sentence, she would get confused and could not remember the stimulus word. A subsequent analysis of her errors revealed that she would begin with letters that came from the first word in the sentence because she had lost the stimulus word. She would prefer to have the word in isolation, even if it was a word with more than one meaning. When spelling a homonym, her chances were better if the word were in isolation, for she at least had a 50/50 chance of being correct.

## Summary

Teaching to modality strengths is an approach to instruction that has potential applications at all levels of instruction, from the elementary grades through post-secondary programs. Basic skills such as reading, writing, and arithmetic can be taught through modality-based instruction, as can content areas such as science and social studies. Without a doubt, modality-based instruction is a powerful educational tool.

There are two forms that modality-based instruction takes. When presenting a lesson for the first time, modality-based instruction provides a framework within which the teacher can design instructional strategies. When initial presentation of a lesson has not succeeded, or in remedial situations, teaching to modality strengths has a better probability of success than other didactic techniques, principally because learning strengths rather than areas of deficiency are emphasized. The *point of intervention* is the term used to describe the point at which initial teaching has not brought about learning for one or more students. The teacher must present the lesson again, this time capitalizing on the particular modality strength of the student. At the point of intervention, the teacher may revert to grouping, or providing self-instructional materials.

## References

Barbe, W.B. and Lucas, V.H. *Barbe-Lucas Handwriting Skill-Guide Check List*. Columbus, Ohio: Zaner-Bloser, 1978.

Bloom, B.S. (Ed.) *Taxonomy of educational objectives. Handbook I: Cognitive domain*. New York: McKay, 1956.

Pearson, C. Do you know how to Chisanbop? *Learning*, 1978, 7, 134–138.

# CHAPTER VI

# Summary

This closing chapter will highlight the most important concepts associated with modality-based instruction. These concepts include: the definitions of modality and modality strengths, the measurement of these strengths, modality-based instruction and its history. In addition to summarizing these concepts, we will discuss the promise modality-based instruction holds for teachers and students.

### The Definition of Modality

The modalities are the channels through which individuals receive and retain information, and comprise three elements—sensation, perception, and memory. The educationally relevant modalities are the visual, auditory, and kinesthetic. The first two of these correspond to the senses of vision and audition, but the third is more than simply the sense of touch, and consists of large muscle, small muscle, and tactile abilities.

### Modality Strengths

If an individual is able to process information more efficiently through one of the modalities, then that person is said to have a dominant modality or a modality strength. A person may also have a secondary modality, one that is not so strong as the dominant modality, but which can serve to process information when the person is unable to do so through the dominant modality. If any two or all three of the educationally relevant modalities are equally strong, the person is said to have a mixed modality strength.

### Measuring Modality Strengths

The way that modality strength is defined determines how it is measured. If modality strength is seen as a fixed neurological characteristic that is solely a function of heredity, then it is equated with sensation, and is measured in terms of the efficiency of the pathway between the organ of sensation and the brain center in which the sensation is processed. This perspective on modality is the most fundamental, but is reductionist in that it ignores the influence of learning on human behavior and development.

To some, modality strengths are the same as modality preferences. Measurement, then, entails simply self-report: the individual indicates the modality with which he or she is most comfortable. Unfortunately, there is no guarantee that the modality an individual favors is the modality through which information is processed most efficiently.

A third definition of modality strength, the one to which we subscribe, is based on a person's ability to perform an educationally relevant task, and comprises sensation, perception, and memory. The Swassing-Barbe Modality Index measures modality strength as it is thus defined: the individual is presented with a stimulus, a sequence of familiar shapes, and is asked to reconstruct the sequence. The stimulus is presented through each of the modalities; the strongest modality is the one in which the task is completed most efficiently. This measurement system produces percentage scores in each modality, thereby allowing intraindividual comparisons but preventing interindividual comparisons.

## Modality-Based Instruction

When a teacher organizes lessons around the modality strengths of students, that teacher is practicing modality-based instruction. Modality-based instruction takes two forms: initial teaching strategies and strategies that are used when a child fails to grasp a basic skill as it is first presented. The time at which this failure is noted is called the point of intervention. At this point, the teacher may group children with similar modality strengths for supplemental instruction or refer children to self-instructional activities.

Teachers should be aware that they, too, have modality strengths and are probably already organizing their teaching around their own area of strength. There is nothing wrong with this tendency, as long as the teacher is willing and able to adapt his or her instructional style to accommodate those children with learning strengths other than the teacher's.

Modality-based instruction can be undertaken at all levels of schooling. It is of greatest value in teaching basic skills, but can also be applied to instruction in the content areas. Since modality-based instruction is strength-oriented, teachers can expect students to learn rapidly and enjoy doing it.

## The History of Modality-Based Instruction

The use of all the educationally relevant modalities to teach writing and reading dates as far back as pre-Christian Greece and Rome. It was not until the mid-eighteenth century, however, that relying upon the senses for educational purposes became popularized. At that time, the philosophers Rousseau and Condillac promoted sensory education as the means of achieving the full potential of human beings. Their theories were applied by several educators, most notably Itard, who attempted to instruct Victor, the Wild Boy of Aveyron, in the rudiments of reading and writing. Itard's methods were extended by Seguin to teaching mentally retarded individuals. Several decades later, at the beginning of the twentieth century, Maria Montessori built her method upon the foundation established by Itard and Seguin.

Soon after Montessori's method had been acclaimed on the Continent, Grace Fernald began using a multisensory approach in the United States. Her contemporary, Samuel Orton, resorted to similar tactics in working with children who had learning problems. Strauss, Kephart, and Lehtinen followed the lead of Orton and Fernald and applied their knowledge of sensory processing to teaching brain-injured children.

Education based upon a diagnosis of perceptual characteristics was developed by Kirk for use with learning-disabled children. Frostig approached the problem in much the same way, but emphasized visual perception. Kirk, Frostig, and others who worked with learning-disabled children set the stage for the contemporary educators who are extending the application of modality-based instruction to the general school population.

## The Promise of Modality-Based Instruction

The promise modality-based instruction holds for each child is that achievement will be consonant with ability. Success rather than failure is promoted, and students are allowed to progress at their own rate. The need for acquiring isolated and perhaps irrelevant skills is eliminated, and application rather than mere understanding is emphasized.

73

## SUMMARY

Modality-based instruction offers a teacher the opportunity to function uniquely. Instead of trying to become like some other teacher, each individual can work in the areas of her or his own strength, understanding why success is more likely with one student than another, why the use of certain types of teaching aids are preferred over others, and why teaching strategies that are so successful for one teacher are not so successful for another. The promise of modality-based instruction for each of us as teachers is that it allows us to be successful in our area of strength, without condemning us for problems in areas of weakness.

The teacher who understands the concept of modality strengths may better understand why teaching was chosen as a profession in the first place, why a particular college major was selected, and why certain reading materials are preferred. The means we choose to communicate to others may become clear, as may the reason that communicating with some people is difficult.

Once an understanding of modality strengths is gained, it is likely that a better relationship with parents can be established. Communication will be enhanced, and the teacher will be able to help parents understand their children better. And, no matter what the circumstance, knowing the child's modality strength will always give the teacher a positive approach to a student.

Through an understanding and application of the principles of modality, the relationship between teachers and their colleagues will be enriched. Just as each teacher has a modality strength that is reflected in day-to-day teaching, so also do supervisors. Supervisory personnel are influenced by their modality strengths in not so subtle ways: the visual supervisor will urge more displays within the classroom, the auditory supervisor more audio equipment, and the kinesthetic supervisor more experiential learning. The teacher should not interpret these recommendations as an indictment of his or her teaching; they merely reflect the modality strength of the supervisor.

Finally, modality-based instruction promises to respond to the increased demands society has placed upon the schools. In years past, student learning was the foremost concern of educators; the cost involved was not a primary consideration. Today, however, it is not enough to educate children; it must be done with a minimal expenditure of resources.

74

Modality-based instruction is a method of teaching that reflects the two major concerns of educators. It is *effective* in that it capitalizes upon children's strengths to accomplish the primary goal of education. Just as importantly, it is *efficient,* and does so with a minimum of expense. Modality-based instruction, therefore, promotes learning in a way that is consistent with the demands that will characterize education in the 1980s.

# Appendices

# Conversion Table

Raw Scores are converted into percentages by finding the Total Number Correct in the left-hand column and reading across to the column for the Number Correct on Subtest. For example, if the Total Number Correct is 58 and the Number Correct on the Auditory Subtest is 14, the Auditory Percentage would be 24.14%.

## CONVERSION TABLE: RAW SCORES INTO PERCENTAGES

| Total Number Correct | Number Correct on Subtest (Visual, Auditory, or Kinesthetic) | | | | | | | | | | | | | | |
|---|---|---|---|---|---|---|---|---|---|---|---|---|---|---|---|
| | 1 | 2 | 3 | 4 | 5 | 6 | 7 | 8 | 9 | 10 | 11 | 12 | 13 | 14 | 15 |
| 1 | 100.00 | | | | | | | | | | | | | | |
| 2 | 50.00 | 100.00 | | | | | | | | | | | | | |
| 3 | 33.33 | 66.67 | 100.00 | | | | | | | | | | | | |
| 4 | 25.00 | 50.00 | 75.00 | 100.00 | | | | | | | | | | | |
| 5 | 20.00 | 40.00 | 60.00 | 80.00 | 100.00 | | | | | | | | | | |
| 6 | 16.67 | 33.33 | 50.00 | 66.67 | 83.33 | 100.00 | | | | | | | | | |
| 7 | 14.29 | 28.57 | 42.86 | 57.14 | 71.43 | 85.71 | 100.00 | | | | | | | | |
| 8 | 12.50 | 25.00 | 37.50 | 50.00 | 62.50 | 75.00 | 87.50 | 100.00 | | | | | | | |
| 9 | 11.11 | 22.22 | 33.33 | 44.44 | 55.56 | 66.67 | 77.78 | 88.89 | 100.00 | | | | | | |
| 10 | 10.00 | 20.00 | 30.00 | 40.00 | 50.00 | 60.00 | 70.00 | 80.00 | 90.00 | 100.00 | | | | | |
| 11 | 9.09 | 18.18 | 27.27 | 36.36 | 45.45 | 54.55 | 63.64 | 72.73 | 81.82 | 90.91 | 100.00 | | | | |
| 12 | 8.33 | 16.67 | 25.00 | 33.33 | 41.67 | 50.00 | 58.33 | 66.67 | 75.00 | 83.33 | 91.67 | 100.00 | | | |
| 13 | 7.69 | 15.38 | 23.08 | 30.77 | 38.46 | 46.15 | 53.85 | 61.54 | 69.23 | 76.92 | 84.62 | 92.31 | 100.00 | | |
| 14 | 7.14 | 14.29 | 21.43 | 28.57 | 35.71 | 42.86 | 50.00 | 57.14 | 64.29 | 71.43 | 78.57 | 85.71 | 92.86 | 100.00 | |
| 15 | 6.67 | 13.33 | 20.00 | 26.67 | 33.33 | 40.00 | 46.67 | 53.33 | 60.00 | 66.67 | 73.33 | 80.00 | 86.67 | 93.33 | 100.00 |
| 16 | 6.25 | 12.50 | 18.75 | 25.00 | 31.25 | 37.50 | 43.75 | 50.00 | 56.25 | 62.50 | 68.75 | 75.00 | 81.25 | 87.50 | 93.75 |
| 17 | 5.88 | 11.76 | 17.65 | 23.53 | 29.41 | 35.29 | 41.18 | 47.06 | 52.94 | 58.82 | 64.71 | 70.59 | 76.47 | 82.35 | 88.24 |
| 18 | 5.56 | 11.11 | 16.67 | 22.22 | 27.78 | 33.33 | 38.89 | 44.44 | 50.00 | 55.56 | 61.11 | 66.67 | 72.22 | 77.78 | 83.33 |
| 19 | 5.26 | 10.53 | 15.79 | 21.05 | 26.32 | 31.58 | 36.84 | 42.11 | 47.37 | 52.63 | 57.89 | 63.16 | 68.42 | 73.68 | 78.95 |
| 20 | 5.00 | 10.00 | 15.00 | 20.00 | 25.00 | 30.00 | 35.00 | 40.00 | 45.00 | 50.00 | 55.00 | 60.00 | 65.00 | 70.00 | 75.00 |
| 21 | 4.76 | 9.52 | 14.29 | 19.05 | 23.81 | 28.57 | 33.33 | 38.10 | 42.86 | 47.62 | 52.38 | 57.14 | 61.90 | 66.67 | 71.43 |
| 22 | 4.55 | 9.09 | 13.64 | 18.18 | 22.73 | 27.27 | 31.82 | 36.36 | 40.91 | 45.45 | 50.00 | 54.55 | 59.09 | 63.64 | 68.18 |
| 23 | 4.35 | 8.70 | 13.04 | 17.39 | 21.74 | 26.09 | 30.43 | 34.78 | 39.13 | 43.48 | 47.83 | 52.17 | 56.52 | 60.87 | 65.22 |
| 24 | 4.17 | 8.33 | 12.50 | 16.67 | 20.83 | 25.00 | 29.17 | 33.33 | 37.50 | 41.67 | 45.83 | 50.00 | 54.17 | 58.33 | 62.50 |
| 25 | 4.00 | 8.00 | 12.00 | 16.00 | 20.00 | 24.00 | 28.00 | 32.00 | 36.00 | 40.00 | 44.00 | 48.00 | 52.00 | 56.00 | 60.00 |
| 26 | 3.85 | 7.69 | 11.54 | 15.38 | 19.23 | 23.08 | 26.92 | 30.77 | 34.62 | 38.46 | 42.31 | 46.15 | 50.00 | 53.85 | 57.69 |
| 27 | 3.70 | 7.41 | 11.11 | 14.81 | 18.52 | 22.22 | 25.93 | 29.63 | 33.33 | 37.04 | 40.74 | 44.44 | 48.15 | 51.85 | 55.56 |
| 28 | 3.57 | 7.14 | 10.71 | 14.29 | 17.86 | 21.43 | 25.00 | 28.57 | 32.14 | 35.71 | 39.29 | 42.86 | 46.43 | 50.00 | 53.57 |
| 29 | 3.45 | 6.90 | 10.34 | 13.79 | 17.24 | 20.69 | 24.14 | 27.59 | 31.03 | 34.48 | 37.93 | 41.38 | 44.83 | 48.28 | 51.72 |
| 30 | 3.33 | 6.67 | 10.00 | 13.33 | 16.67 | 20.00 | 23.33 | 26.67 | 30.00 | 33.33 | 36.67 | 40.00 | 43.33 | 46.67 | 50.00 |
| 31 | 3.23 | 6.45 | 9.68 | 12.90 | 16.13 | 19.35 | 22.58 | 25.81 | 29.03 | 32.26 | 35.48 | 38.71 | 41.94 | 45.16 | 48.39 |
| 32 | 3.13 | 6.25 | 9.38 | 12.50 | 15.63 | 18.75 | 21.88 | 25.00 | 28.13 | 31.25 | 34.38 | 37.50 | 40.63 | 43.75 | 46.88 |
| 33 | 3.03 | 6.06 | 9.09 | 12.12 | 15.15 | 18.18 | 21.21 | 24.24 | 27.27 | 30.30 | 33.33 | 36.36 | 39.39 | 42.42 | 45.45 |
| 34 | 2.94 | 5.88 | 8.82 | 11.76 | 14.71 | 17.65 | 20.59 | 23.53 | 26.47 | 29.41 | 32.35 | 35.29 | 38.24 | 41.18 | 44.12 |
| 35 | 2.86 | 5.71 | 8.57 | 11.43 | 14.29 | 17.14 | 20.00 | 22.86 | 25.71 | 28.57 | 31.43 | 34.29 | 37.14 | 40.00 | 42.86 |
| 36 | 2.78 | 5.56 | 8.33 | 11.11 | 13.89 | 16.67 | 19.44 | 22.22 | 25.00 | 27.78 | 30.56 | 33.33 | 36.11 | 38.89 | 41.67 |
| 37 | 2.70 | 5.41 | 8.11 | 10.81 | 13.51 | 16.22 | 18.92 | 21.62 | 24.32 | 27.03 | 29.73 | 32.43 | 35.14 | 37.94 | 40.54 |
| 38 | 2.63 | 5.26 | 7.89 | 10.53 | 13.16 | 15.79 | 18.42 | 21.05 | 23.68 | 26.32 | 28.95 | 31.58 | 34.21 | 36.84 | 39.47 |
| 39 | 2.56 | 5.13 | 7.69 | 10.26 | 12.82 | 15.38 | 17.95 | 20.51 | 23.08 | 25.64 | 28.21 | 30.77 | 33.33 | 35.90 | 38.46 |
| 40 | 2.50 | 5.00 | 7.50 | 10.00 | 12.50 | 15.00 | 17.50 | 20.00 | 22.50 | 25.00 | 27.50 | 30.00 | 32.50 | 35.00 | 37.50 |
| 41 | 2.44 | 4.88 | 7.32 | 9.76 | 12.20 | 14.63 | 17.07 | 19.51 | 21.95 | 24.39 | 26.83 | 29.27 | 31.71 | 34.15 | 36.59 |
| 42 | 2.38 | 4.76 | 7.14 | 9.52 | 11.90 | 14.29 | 16.67 | 19.05 | 21.43 | 23.81 | 26.19 | 28.57 | 30.95 | 33.33 | 35.71 |
| 43 | 2.33 | 4.65 | 6.98 | 9.30 | 11.63 | 13.95 | 16.28 | 18.60 | 20.93 | 23.26 | 25.58 | 27.91 | 30.23 | 32.56 | 34.88 |
| 44 | 2.27 | 4.55 | 6.82 | 9.09 | 11.36 | 13.64 | 15.91 | 18.18 | 20.45 | 22.73 | 25.00 | 27.27 | 29.55 | 31.82 | 34.09 |
| 45 | 2.22 | 4.44 | 6.67 | 8.89 | 11.11 | 13.33 | 15.56 | 17.78 | 20.00 | 22.22 | 24.44 | 26.67 | 28.89 | 31.11 | 33.33 |
| 46 | 2.17 | 4.35 | 6.52 | 8.70 | 10.87 | 13.04 | 15.22 | 17.39 | 19.57 | 21.74 | 23.91 | 26.09 | 28.26 | 30.43 | 32.61 |
| 47 | 2.13 | 4.26 | 6.38 | 8.51 | 10.64 | 12.77 | 14.89 | 17.02 | 19.15 | 21.28 | 23.40 | 25.53 | 27.66 | 29.79 | 31.91 |
| 48 | 2.08 | 4.17 | 6.25 | 8.33 | 10.42 | 12.50 | 14.58 | 16.67 | 18.75 | 20.83 | 22.92 | 25.00 | 27.08 | 29.17 | 31.25 |
| 49 | 2.04 | 4.08 | 6.12 | 8.16 | 10.20 | 12.24 | 14.29 | 16.33 | 18.37 | 20.41 | 22.45 | 24.49 | 26.53 | 28.57 | 30.61 |
| 50 | 2.00 | 4.00 | 6.00 | 8.00 | 10.00 | 12.00 | 14.00 | 16.00 | 18.00 | 20.00 | 22.00 | 24.00 | 26.00 | 28.00 | 30.00 |
| 51 | 1.96 | 3.92 | 5.88 | 7.84 | 9.80 | 11.76 | 13.73 | 15.69 | 17.65 | 19.61 | 21.57 | 23.53 | 25.49 | 27.45 | 29.41 |
| 52 | 1.92 | 3.85 | 5.77 | 7.69 | 9.62 | 11.54 | 13.46 | 15.38 | 17.31 | 19.23 | 21.15 | 23.08 | 25.00 | 26.92 | 28.85 |
| 53 | 1.89 | 3.77 | 5.66 | 7.55 | 9.43 | 11.32 | 13.21 | 15.09 | 16.98 | 18.87 | 20.75 | 22.64 | 24.53 | 26.42 | 28.30 |
| 54 | 1.85 | 3.70 | 5.56 | 7.41 | 9.26 | 11.11 | 12.96 | 14.81 | 16.67 | 18.52 | 20.37 | 22.22 | 24.07 | 25.93 | 27.78 |
| 55 | 1.82 | 3.64 | 5.45 | 7.27 | 9.09 | 10.91 | 12.73 | 14.55 | 16.36 | 18.18 | 20.00 | 21.82 | 23.64 | 25.45 | 27.27 |
| 56 | 1.79 | 3.57 | 5.36 | 7.14 | 8.93 | 10.71 | 12.50 | 14.29 | 16.07 | 17.86 | 19.64 | 21.43 | 23.21 | 25.00 | 26.79 |
| 57 | 1.75 | 3.51 | 5.26 | 7.02 | 8.77 | 10.53 | 12.28 | 14.04 | 15.79 | 17.54 | 19.30 | 21.05 | 22.81 | 24.56 | 26.32 |
| 58 | 1.72 | 3.45 | 5.17 | 6.90 | 8.62 | 10.34 | 12.07 | 13.79 | 15.52 | 17.24 | 18.97 | 20.69 | 22.41 | 24.14 | 25.86 |
| 59 | 1.69 | 3.39 | 5.08 | 6.78 | 8.47 | 10.17 | 11.86 | 13.56 | 15.25 | 16.95 | 18.64 | 20.34 | 22.03 | 23.73 | 25.42 |
| 60 | 1.67 | 3.33 | 5.00 | 6.67 | 8.33 | 10.00 | 11.67 | 13.33 | 15.00 | 16.67 | 18.33 | 20.00 | 21.67 | 23.33 | 25.00 |

| Total Number Correct | Number Correct on Subtest (Visual, Auditory, or Kinesthetic) | | | | | | | | | | | | | | |
|---|---|---|---|---|---|---|---|---|---|---|---|---|---|---|---|
| | 1 | 2 | 3 | 4 | 5 | 6 | 7 | 8 | 9 | 10 | 11 | 12 | 13 | 14 | 15 |
| 61 | 1.64 | 3.28 | 4.92 | 6.56 | 8.20 | 9.84 | 11.48 | 13.11 | 14.75 | 16.39 | 18.03 | 19.67 | 21.31 | 22.95 | 24.59 |
| 62 | 1.61 | 3.23 | 4.84 | 6.45 | 8.06 | 9.68 | 11.29 | 12.90 | 14.52 | 16.13 | 17.74 | 19.35 | 20.97 | 22.58 | 24.19 |
| 63 | 1.59 | 3.17 | 4.76 | 6.35 | 7.94 | 9.52 | 11.11 | 12.70 | 14.29 | 15.87 | 17.46 | 19.05 | 20.63 | 22.22 | 23.81 |
| 64 | 1.56 | 3.13 | 4.69 | 6.25 | 7.81 | 9.38 | 10.94 | 12.50 | 14.06 | 15.63 | 17.19 | 18.75 | 20.31 | 21.88 | 23.44 |
| 65 | 1.54 | 3.08 | 4.62 | 6.15 | 7.69 | 9.23 | 10.77 | 12.31 | 13.85 | 15.38 | 16.92 | 18.46 | 20.00 | 21.54 | 23.08 |
| 66 | 1.52 | 3.03 | 4.55 | 6.06 | 7.58 | 9.09 | 10.61 | 12.12 | 13.64 | 15.15 | 16.67 | 18.18 | 19.70 | 21.21 | 22.73 |
| 67 | 1.49 | 2.99 | 4.48 | 5.97 | 7.46 | 8.96 | 10.45 | 11.94 | 13.43 | 14.93 | 16.42 | 17.91 | 19.40 | 20.90 | 22.39 |
| 68 | 1.47 | 2.94 | 4.41 | 5.88 | 7.35 | 8.82 | 10.29 | 11.76 | 13.24 | 14.71 | 16.18 | 17.65 | 19.12 | 20.59 | 22.06 |
| 69 | 1.45 | 2.90 | 4.35 | 5.80 | 7.25 | 8.70 | 10.14 | 11.59 | 13.04 | 14.49 | 15.94 | 17.39 | 18.84 | 20.29 | 21.74 |
| 70 | 1.43 | 2.86 | 4.29 | 5.71 | 7.14 | 8.57 | 10.00 | 11.43 | 12.86 | 14.29 | 15.71 | 17.14 | 18.57 | 20.00 | 21.43 |
| 71 | 1.41 | 2.82 | 4.23 | 5.63 | 7.04 | 8.45 | 9.86 | 11.27 | 12.68 | 14.08 | 15.49 | 16.90 | 18.31 | 19.72 | 21.13 |
| 72 | 1.39 | 2.78 | 4.17 | 5.56 | 6.94 | 8.33 | 9.72 | 11.11 | 12.50 | 13.89 | 15.28 | 16.67 | 18.06 | 19.44 | 20.83 |
| 73 | 1.37 | 2.74 | 4.11 | 5.48 | 6.85 | 8.22 | 9.59 | 10.96 | 12.33 | 13.70 | 15.07 | 16.44 | 17.81 | 19.18 | 20.55 |
| 74 | 1.35 | 2.70 | 4.05 | 5.41 | 6.76 | 8.11 | 9.46 | 10.81 | 12.16 | 13.51 | 14.86 | 16.22 | 17.57 | 18.92 | 20.27 |
| 75 | 1.33 | 2.67 | 4.00 | 5.33 | 6.67 | 8.00 | 9.33 | 10.67 | 12.00 | 13.33 | 14.67 | 16.00 | 17.33 | 18.67 | 20.00 |
| 76 | 1.32 | 2.63 | 3.95 | 5.26 | 6.58 | 7.89 | 9.21 | 10.53 | 11.84 | 13.16 | 14.47 | 15.79 | 17.11 | 18.42 | 19.74 |
| 77 | 1.30 | 2.60 | 3.90 | 5.19 | 6.49 | 7.79 | 9.09 | 10.39 | 11.69 | 12.99 | 14.29 | 15.58 | 16.88 | 18.18 | 19.48 |
| 78 | 1.28 | 2.56 | 3.85 | 5.13 | 6.41 | 7.69 | 8.97 | 10.26 | 11.54 | 12.82 | 14.10 | 15.38 | 16.67 | 17.95 | 19.23 |
| 79 | 1.27 | 2.53 | 3.80 | 5.06 | 6.33 | 7.59 | 8.86 | 10.13 | 11.39 | 12.66 | 13.92 | 15.19 | 16.46 | 17.72 | 18.99 |
| 80 | 1.25 | 2.50 | 3.75 | 5.00 | 6.25 | 7.50 | 8.75 | 10.00 | 11.25 | 12.50 | 13.75 | 15.00 | 16.25 | 17.50 | 18.75 |
| 81 | 1.23 | 2.47 | 3.70 | 4.94 | 6.17 | 7.41 | 8.64 | 9.88 | 11.11 | 12.35 | 13.58 | 14.81 | 16.05 | 17.28 | 18.52 |
| 82 | 1.22 | 2.44 | 3.66 | 4.88 | 6.10 | 7.32 | 8.54 | 9.76 | 10.98 | 12.20 | 13.41 | 14.63 | 15.85 | 17.07 | 18.29 |
| 83 | 1.20 | 2.41 | 3.61 | 4.82 | 6.02 | 7.23 | 8.43 | 9.64 | 10.84 | 12.05 | 13.25 | 14.46 | 15.66 | 16.87 | 18.07 |
| 84 | 1.19 | 2.38 | 3.57 | 4.76 | 5.95 | 7.14 | 8.33 | 9.52 | 10.71 | 11.90 | 13.10 | 14.29 | 15.48 | 16.67 | 17.86 |
| 85 | 1.18 | 2.35 | 3.53 | 4.71 | 5.88 | 7.06 | 8.24 | 9.41 | 10.59 | 11.76 | 12.94 | 14.12 | 15.29 | 16.47 | 17.65 |
| 86 | 1.16 | 2.33 | 3.49 | 4.65 | 5.81 | 6.98 | 8.14 | 9.30 | 10.47 | 11.63 | 12.79 | 13.95 | 15.12 | 16.28 | 17.44 |
| 87 | 1.15 | 2.30 | 3.45 | 4.60 | 5.75 | 6.90 | 8.05 | 9.20 | 10.34 | 11.49 | 12.64 | 13.79 | 14.94 | 16.09 | 17.24 |
| 88 | 1.14 | 2.27 | 3.41 | 4.55 | 5.68 | 6.82 | 7.95 | 9.09 | 10.23 | 11.36 | 12.50 | 13.64 | 14.77 | 15.91 | 17.05 |
| 89 | 1.12 | 2.25 | 3.37 | 4.49 | 5.62 | 6.74 | 7.87 | 8.99 | 10.11 | 11.24 | 12.36 | 13.48 | 14.61 | 15.73 | 16.85 |
| 90 | 1.11 | 2.22 | 3.33 | 4.44 | 5.56 | 6.67 | 7.78 | 8.89 | 10.00 | 11.11 | 12.22 | 13.33 | 14.44 | 15.56 | 16.67 |
| 91 | 1.10 | 2.20 | 3.30 | 4.40 | 5.49 | 6.59 | 7.69 | 8.79 | 9.89 | 10.99 | 12.09 | 13.19 | 14.29 | 15.38 | 16.48 |
| 92 | 1.09 | 2.17 | 3.26 | 4.35 | 5.43 | 6.52 | 7.61 | 8.70 | 9.78 | 10.87 | 11.96 | 13.04 | 14.13 | 15.22 | 16.30 |
| 93 | 1.08 | 2.15 | 3.23 | 4.30 | 5.38 | 6.45 | 7.53 | 8.60 | 9.68 | 10.75 | 11.83 | 12.90 | 13.98 | 15.05 | 16.13 |
| 94 | 1.06 | 2.13 | 3.19 | 4.26 | 5.32 | 6.38 | 7.45 | 8.51 | 9.57 | 10.64 | 11.70 | 12.77 | 13.83 | 14.89 | 15.96 |
| 95 | 1.05 | 2.11 | 3.16 | 4.21 | 5.26 | 6.32 | 7.37 | 8.42 | 9.47 | 10.53 | 11.58 | 12.63 | 13.68 | 14.74 | 15.79 |
| 96 | 1.04 | 2.08 | 3.13 | 4.17 | 5.21 | 6.25 | 7.29 | 8.33 | 9.38 | 10.42 | 11.46 | 12.50 | 13.54 | 14.58 | 15.63 |
| 97 | 1.03 | 2.06 | 3.09 | 4.12 | 5.15 | 6.19 | 7.22 | 8.25 | 9.28 | 10.31 | 11.34 | 12.37 | 13.40 | 14.43 | 15.46 |
| 98 | 1.02 | 2.04 | 3.06 | 4.08 | 5.10 | 6.12 | 7.14 | 8.16 | 9.18 | 10.20 | 11.22 | 12.24 | 13.27 | 14.29 | 15.31 |
| 99 | 1.01 | 2.02 | 3.03 | 4.04 | 5.05 | 6.06 | 7.07 | 8.08 | 9.09 | 10.10 | 11.11 | 12.12 | 13.13 | 14.14 | 15.15 |
| 100 | 1.00 | 2.00 | 3.00 | 4.00 | 5.00 | 6.00 | 7.00 | 8.00 | 9.00 | 10.00 | 11.00 | 12.00 | 13.00 | 14.00 | 15.00 |
| 101 | 0.99 | 1.98 | 2.97 | 3.96 | 4.95 | 5.94 | 6.93 | 7.92 | 8.91 | 9.90 | 10.89 | 11.88 | 12.87 | 13.86 | 14.85 |
| 102 | 0.98 | 1.96 | 2.94 | 3.92 | 4.90 | 5.88 | 6.86 | 7.84 | 8.82 | 9.80 | 10.78 | 11.76 | 12.75 | 13.73 | 14.71 |
| 103 | 0.97 | 1.94 | 2.91 | 3.88 | 4.85 | 5.83 | 6.80 | 7.77 | 8.74 | 9.71 | 10.68 | 11.65 | 12.62 | 13.59 | 14.56 |
| 104 | 0.96 | 1.92 | 2.88 | 3.85 | 4.81 | 5.77 | 6.73 | 7.69 | 8.65 | 9.62 | 10.58 | 11.54 | 12.50 | 13.46 | 14.42 |
| 105 | 0.95 | 1.90 | 2.86 | 3.81 | 4.76 | 5.71 | 6.67 | 7.62 | 8.57 | 9.52 | 10.48 | 11.43 | 12.38 | 13.33 | 14.29 |
| 106 | 0.94 | 1.89 | 2.83 | 3.77 | 4.72 | 5.66 | 6.60 | 7.55 | 8.49 | 9.43 | 10.38 | 11.32 | 12.26 | 13.21 | 14.15 |
| 107 | 0.93 | 1.87 | 2.80 | 3.74 | 4.67 | 5.61 | 6.54 | 7.48 | 8.41 | 9.35 | 10.28 | 11.21 | 12.15 | 13.08 | 14.02 |
| 108 | 0.93 | 1.85 | 2.78 | 3.70 | 4.63 | 5.56 | 6.48 | 7.41 | 8.33 | 9.26 | 10.19 | 11.11 | 12.04 | 12.96 | 13.89 |
| 109 | 0.92 | 1.83 | 2.75 | 3.67 | 4.59 | 5.50 | 6.42 | 7.34 | 8.26 | 9.17 | 10.09 | 11.01 | 11.93 | 12.84 | 13.76 |
| 110 | 0.91 | 1.82 | 2.73 | 3.64 | 4.55 | 5.45 | 6.36 | 7.27 | 8.18 | 9.09 | 10.00 | 10.91 | 11.82 | 12.73 | 13.64 |
| 111 | 0.90 | 1.80 | 2.70 | 3.60 | 4.50 | 5.41 | 6.31 | 7.21 | 8.11 | 9.01 | 9.91 | 10.81 | 11.71 | 12.61 | 13.51 |
| 112 | 0.89 | 1.79 | 2.68 | 3.57 | 4.46 | 5.36 | 6.25 | 7.14 | 8.04 | 8.93 | 9.82 | 10.71 | 11.61 | 12.50 | 13.39 |
| 113 | 0.88 | 1.77 | 2.65 | 3.54 | 4.42 | 5.31 | 6.19 | 7.08 | 7.96 | 8.85 | 9.73 | 10.62 | 11.50 | 12.39 | 13.27 |
| 114 | 0.88 | 1.75 | 2.63 | 3.51 | 4.39 | 5.26 | 6.14 | 7.02 | 7.89 | 8.77 | 9.65 | 10.53 | 11.40 | 12.28 | 13.16 |
| 115 | 0.87 | 1.74 | 2.61 | 3.48 | 4.35 | 5.22 | 6.09 | 6.96 | 7.83 | 8.70 | 9.57 | 10.43 | 11.30 | 12.17 | 13.04 |
| 116 | 0.86 | 1.72 | 2.59 | 3.45 | 4.31 | 5.17 | 6.03 | 6.90 | 7.76 | 8.62 | 9.48 | 10.34 | 11.21 | 12.07 | 12.93 |
| 117 | 0.85 | 1.71 | 2.56 | 3.42 | 4.27 | 5.13 | 5.98 | 6.84 | 7.69 | 8.55 | 9.40 | 10.26 | 11.11 | 11.97 | 12.82 |
| 118 | 0.85 | 1.69 | 2.54 | 3.39 | 4.24 | 5.08 | 5.93 | 6.78 | 7.63 | 8.47 | 9.32 | 10.17 | 11.02 | 11.86 | 12.71 |
| 119 | 0.84 | 1.68 | 2.52 | 3.36 | 4.20 | 5.04 | 5.88 | 6.72 | 7.56 | 8.40 | 9.24 | 10.08 | 10.92 | 11.76 | 12.61 |
| 120 | 0.83 | 1.67 | 2.50 | 3.33 | 4.17 | 5.00 | 5.83 | 6.67 | 7.50 | 8.33 | 9.17 | 10.00 | 10.83 | 11.67 | 12.50 |
| 121 | 0.83 | 1.65 | 2.48 | 3.31 | 4.13 | 4.96 | 5.79 | 6.61 | 7.44 | 8.26 | 9.09 | 9.92 | 10.74 | 11.57 | 12.40 |
| 122 | 0.82 | 1.64 | 2.46 | 3.28 | 4.10 | 4.92 | 5.74 | 6.56 | 7.38 | 8.20 | 9.02 | 9.84 | 10.66 | 11.48 | 12.30 |
| 123 | 0.81 | 1.63 | 2.44 | 3.25 | 4.07 | 4.88 | 5.69 | 6.50 | 7.32 | 8.13 | 8.94 | 9.76 | 10.57 | 11.38 | 12.20 |
| 124 | 0.81 | 1.61 | 2.42 | 3.23 | 4.03 | 4.84 | 5.65 | 6.45 | 7.26 | 8.06 | 8.87 | 9.68 | 10.48 | 11.29 | 12.10 |
| 125 | 0.80 | 1.60 | 2.40 | 3.20 | 4.00 | 4.80 | 5.60 | 6.40 | 7.20 | 8.00 | 8.80 | 9.60 | 10.40 | 11.20 | 12.00 |
| 126 | 0.79 | 1.59 | 2.38 | 3.17 | 3.97 | 4.76 | 5.56 | 6.35 | 7.14 | 7.94 | 8.73 | 9.52 | 10.32 | 11.11 | 11.90 |
| 127 | 0.79 | 1.57 | 2.36 | 3.15 | 3.94 | 4.72 | 5.51 | 6.30 | 7.09 | 7.87 | 8.66 | 9.45 | 10.24 | 11.02 | 11.81 |
| 128 | 0.78 | 1.56 | 2.34 | 3.13 | 3.91 | 4.69 | 5.47 | 6.25 | 7.03 | 7.81 | 8.59 | 9.38 | 10.16 | 10.94 | 11.72 |
| 129 | 0.78 | 1.55 | 2.33 | 3.10 | 3.88 | 4.65 | 5.43 | 6.20 | 6.98 | 7.75 | 8.53 | 9.30 | 10.08 | 10.85 | 11.63 |
| 130 | 0.77 | 1.54 | 2.31 | 3.08 | 3.85 | 4.62 | 5.38 | 6.15 | 6.92 | 7.69 | 8.46 | 9.23 | 10.00 | 10.77 | 11.54 |
| 131 | 0.76 | 1.53 | 2.29 | 3.05 | 3.82 | 4.58 | 5.34 | 6.11 | 6.87 | 7.63 | 8.40 | 9.16 | 9.92 | 10.69 | 11.45 |
| 132 | 0.76 | 1.52 | 2.27 | 3.03 | 3.79 | 4.55 | 5.30 | 6.06 | 6.82 | 7.58 | 8.33 | 9.09 | 9.85 | 10.61 | 11.36 |
| 133 | 0.75 | 1.50 | 2.26 | 3.01 | 3.76 | 4.51 | 5.26 | 6.02 | 6.77 | 7.52 | 8.27 | 9.02 | 9.77 | 10.53 | 11.28 |
| 134 | 0.75 | 1.49 | 2.24 | 2.99 | 3.73 | 4.48 | 5.22 | 5.97 | 6.72 | 7.46 | 8.21 | 8.96 | 9.70 | 10.45 | 11.19 |
| 135 | 0.74 | 1.48 | 2.22 | 2.96 | 3.70 | 4.44 | 5.19 | 5.93 | 6.67 | 7.41 | 8.15 | 8.89 | 9.63 | 10.37 | 11.11 |

| Total Number Correct | Number Correct on Subtest (Visual, Auditory, or Kinesthetic) | | | | | | | | | | | | | | |
|---|---|---|---|---|---|---|---|---|---|---|---|---|---|---|---|
| | 16 | 17 | 18 | 19 | 20 | 21 | 22 | 23 | 24 | 25 | 26 | 27 | 28 | 29 | 30 |
| 16 | 100.00 | | | | | | | | | | | | | | |
| 17 | 94.12 | 100.00 | | | | | | | | | | | | | |
| 18 | 88.89 | 94.44 | 100.00 | | | | | | | | | | | | |
| 19 | 84.21 | 89.47 | 94.74 | 100.00 | | | | | | | | | | | |
| 20 | 80.00 | 85.00 | 90.00 | 95.00 | 100.00 | | | | | | | | | | |
| 21 | 76.19 | 80.95 | 85.71 | 90.48 | 95.24 | 100.00 | | | | | | | | | |
| 22 | 72.73 | 77.27 | 81.82 | 86.36 | 90.91 | 95.45 | 100.00 | | | | | | | | |
| 23 | 69.57 | 73.91 | 78.26 | 82.61 | 86.96 | 91.30 | 95.65 | 100.00 | | | | | | | |
| 24 | 66.67 | 70.83 | 75.00 | 79.17 | 83.33 | 87.50 | 91.67 | 95.83 | 100.00 | | | | | | |
| 25 | 64.00 | 68.00 | 72.00 | 76.00 | 80.00 | 84.00 | 88.00 | 92.00 | 96.00 | 100.00 | | | | | |
| 26 | 61.54 | 65.38 | 69.23 | 73.08 | 76.92 | 80.77 | 84.62 | 88.46 | 92.31 | 96.15 | 100.00 | | | | |
| 27 | 59.26 | 62.96 | 66.67 | 70.37 | 74.07 | 77.78 | 81.48 | 85.19 | 88.89 | 92.59 | 96.30 | 100.00 | | | |
| 28 | 57.14 | 60.71 | 64.29 | 67.86 | 71.43 | 75.00 | 78.57 | 82.14 | 85.71 | 89.29 | 92.86 | 96.43 | 100.00 | | |
| 29 | 55.17 | 58.62 | 62.07 | 65.52 | 68.97 | 72.41 | 75.86 | 79.31 | 82.76 | 86.21 | 89.66 | 93.10 | 96.55 | 100.00 | |
| 30 | 53.33 | 56.67 | 60.00 | 63.33 | 66.67 | 70.00 | 73.33 | 76.67 | 80.00 | 83.33 | 86.67 | 90.00 | 93.33 | 96.67 | 100.00 |
| 31 | 51.61 | 54.84 | 58.06 | 61.29 | 64.52 | 67.74 | 70.97 | 74.19 | 77.42 | 80.65 | 83.87 | 87.10 | 90.32 | 93.55 | 96.77 |
| 32 | 50.00 | 53.13 | 56.25 | 59.38 | 62.50 | 65.63 | 68.75 | 71.88 | 75.00 | 78.13 | 81.25 | 84.38 | 87.50 | 90.63 | 93.75 |
| 33 | 48.48 | 51.52 | 54.55 | 57.58 | 60.61 | 63.64 | 66.67 | 69.70 | 72.73 | 75.76 | 78.79 | 81.82 | 84.85 | 87.88 | 90.91 |
| 34 | 47.06 | 50.00 | 52.94 | 55.88 | 58.82 | 61.76 | 64.71 | 67.65 | 70.59 | 73.53 | 76.47 | 79.41 | 82.35 | 85.29 | 88.24 |
| 35 | 45.71 | 48.57 | 51.43 | 54.29 | 57.14 | 60.00 | 62.86 | 65.71 | 68.57 | 71.43 | 74.29 | 77.14 | 80.00 | 82.86 | 85.71 |
| 36 | 44.44 | 47.22 | 50.00 | 52.78 | 55.56 | 58.33 | 61.11 | 63.89 | 66.67 | 69.44 | 72.22 | 75.00 | 77.78 | 80.56 | 83.33 |
| 37 | 43.24 | 45.95 | 48.65 | 51.35 | 54.05 | 56.76 | 59.46 | 62.16 | 64.86 | 67.57 | 70.27 | 72.97 | 75.68 | 78.38 | 81.08 |
| 38 | 42.11 | 44.74 | 47.37 | 50.00 | 52.63 | 55.26 | 57.89 | 60.53 | 63.16 | 65.79 | 68.42 | 71.05 | 73.68 | 76.32 | 78.95 |
| 39 | 41.03 | 43.59 | 46.15 | 48.72 | 51.28 | 53.85 | 56.41 | 58.97 | 61.54 | 64.10 | 66.67 | 69.23 | 71.79 | 74.36 | 76.92 |
| 40 | 40.00 | 42.50 | 45.00 | 47.50 | 50.00 | 52.50 | 55.00 | 57.50 | 60.00 | 62.50 | 65.00 | 67.50 | 70.00 | 72.50 | 75.00 |
| 41 | 39.02 | 41.46 | 43.90 | 46.34 | 48.78 | 51.22 | 53.66 | 56.10 | 58.54 | 60.98 | 63.41 | 65.85 | 68.29 | 70.73 | 73.17 |
| 42 | 38.10 | 40.48 | 42.86 | 45.24 | 47.62 | 50.00 | 52.38 | 54.76 | 57.14 | 59.52 | 61.90 | 64.29 | 66.67 | 69.05 | 71.43 |
| 43 | 37.21 | 39.53 | 41.86 | 44.19 | 46.51 | 48.84 | 51.16 | 53.49 | 55.81 | 58.14 | 60.47 | 62.79 | 65.12 | 67.44 | 69.77 |
| 44 | 36.36 | 38.64 | 40.91 | 43.18 | 45.45 | 47.73 | 50.00 | 52.27 | 54.55 | 56.82 | 59.09 | 61.36 | 63.64 | 65.91 | 68.18 |
| 45 | 35.56 | 37.78 | 40.00 | 42.22 | 44.44 | 46.67 | 48.89 | 51.11 | 53.33 | 55.56 | 57.78 | 60.00 | 62.22 | 64.44 | 66.67 |
| 46 | 34.78 | 36.96 | 39.13 | 41.30 | 43.48 | 45.65 | 47.83 | 50.00 | 52.17 | 54.35 | 56.52 | 58.70 | 60.87 | 63.04 | 65.22 |
| 47 | 34.04 | 36.17 | 38.30 | 40.43 | 42.55 | 44.68 | 46.81 | 48.94 | 51.06 | 53.19 | 55.32 | 57.45 | 59.57 | 61.70 | 63.83 |
| 48 | 33.33 | 35.42 | 37.50 | 39.58 | 41.67 | 43.75 | 45.83 | 47.92 | 50.00 | 52.08 | 54.17 | 56.25 | 58.33 | 60.42 | 62.50 |
| 49 | 32.65 | 34.69 | 36.73 | 38.78 | 40.82 | 42.86 | 44.90 | 46.94 | 48.98 | 51.02 | 53.06 | 55.10 | 57.14 | 59.18 | 61.22 |
| 50 | 32.00 | 34.00 | 36.00 | 38.00 | 40.00 | 42.00 | 44.00 | 46.00 | 48.00 | 50.00 | 52.00 | 54.00 | 56.00 | 58.00 | 60.00 |
| 51 | 31.37 | 33.33 | 35.29 | 37.25 | 39.22 | 41.18 | 43.14 | 45.10 | 47.06 | 49.02 | 50.98 | 52.94 | 54.90 | 56.86 | 58.82 |
| 52 | 30.77 | 32.69 | 34.62 | 36.54 | 38.46 | 40.38 | 42.31 | 44.23 | 46.15 | 48.08 | 50.00 | 51.92 | 53.85 | 55.77 | 57.69 |
| 53 | 30.19 | 32.08 | 33.96 | 35.85 | 37.74 | 39.62 | 41.51 | 43.40 | 45.28 | 47.17 | 49.06 | 50.94 | 52.83 | 54.72 | 56.60 |
| 54 | 29.63 | 31.48 | 33.33 | 35.19 | 37.04 | 38.89 | 40.74 | 42.59 | 44.44 | 46.30 | 48.15 | 50.00 | 51.85 | 53.70 | 55.56 |
| 55 | 29.09 | 30.91 | 32.73 | 34.55 | 36.36 | 38.18 | 40.00 | 41.82 | 43.64 | 45.45 | 47.27 | 49.09 | 50.91 | 52.73 | 54.55 |
| 56 | 28.57 | 30.36 | 32.14 | 33.93 | 35.71 | 37.50 | 39.29 | 41.07 | 42.86 | 44.64 | 46.43 | 48.21 | 50.00 | 51.79 | 53.57 |
| 57 | 28.07 | 29.82 | 31.58 | 33.33 | 35.09 | 36.84 | 38.60 | 40.35 | 42.11 | 43.86 | 45.61 | 47.37 | 49.12 | 50.88 | 52.63 |
| 58 | 27.59 | 29.31 | 31.03 | 32.76 | 34.48 | 36.21 | 37.93 | 39.66 | 41.38 | 43.10 | 44.83 | 46.55 | 48.28 | 50.00 | 51.72 |
| 59 | 27.12 | 28.81 | 30.51 | 32.20 | 33.90 | 35.59 | 37.29 | 38.98 | 40.68 | 42.37 | 44.07 | 45.76 | 47.46 | 49.15 | 50.85 |
| 60 | 26.67 | 28.33 | 30.00 | 31.67 | 33.33 | 35.00 | 36.67 | 38.33 | 40.00 | 41.67 | 43.33 | 45.00 | 46.67 | 48.33 | 50.00 |
| 61 | 26.23 | 27.87 | 29.51 | 31.15 | 32.79 | 34.43 | 36.07 | 37.70 | 39.34 | 40.98 | 42.62 | 44.26 | 45.90 | 47.54 | 49.18 |
| 62 | 25.81 | 27.42 | 29.03 | 30.65 | 32.26 | 33.87 | 35.48 | 37.10 | 38.71 | 40.32 | 41.94 | 43.55 | 45.16 | 46.77 | 48.39 |
| 63 | 25.40 | 26.98 | 28.57 | 30.16 | 31.75 | 33.33 | 34.92 | 36.51 | 38.10 | 39.68 | 41.27 | 42.86 | 44.44 | 46.03 | 47.62 |
| 64 | 25.00 | 26.56 | 28.13 | 29.69 | 31.25 | 32.81 | 34.38 | 35.94 | 37.50 | 39.06 | 40.63 | 42.19 | 43.75 | 45.31 | 46.88 |
| 65 | 24.62 | 26.15 | 27.69 | 29.23 | 30.77 | 32.31 | 33.85 | 35.38 | 36.92 | 38.46 | 40.00 | 41.54 | 43.08 | 44.62 | 46.15 |
| 66 | 24.24 | 25.76 | 27.27 | 28.79 | 30.30 | 31.82 | 33.33 | 34.85 | 36.36 | 37.88 | 39.39 | 40.91 | 42.42 | 43.94 | 45.45 |
| 67 | 23.88 | 25.37 | 26.87 | 28.36 | 29.85 | 31.34 | 32.84 | 34.33 | 35.82 | 37.31 | 38.81 | 40.30 | 41.79 | 43.28 | 44.78 |
| 68 | 23.53 | 25.00 | 26.47 | 27.94 | 29.41 | 30.88 | 32.35 | 33.82 | 35.29 | 36.76 | 38.24 | 39.71 | 41.18 | 42.65 | 44.12 |
| 69 | 23.19 | 24.64 | 26.09 | 27.54 | 28.99 | 30.43 | 31.88 | 33.33 | 34.78 | 36.23 | 37.68 | 39.13 | 40.58 | 42.03 | 43.48 |
| 70 | 22.86 | 24.29 | 25.71 | 27.14 | 28.57 | 30.00 | 31.43 | 32.86 | 34.29 | 35.71 | 37.14 | 38.57 | 40.00 | 41.43 | 42.86 |
| 71 | 22.54 | 23.94 | 25.35 | 26.76 | 28.17 | 29.58 | 30.99 | 32.39 | 33.80 | 35.21 | 36.62 | 38.03 | 39.44 | 40.85 | 42.25 |
| 72 | 22.22 | 23.61 | 25.00 | 26.39 | 27.78 | 29.17 | 30.56 | 31.94 | 33.33 | 34.72 | 36.11 | 37.50 | 38.89 | 40.28 | 41.67 |
| 73 | 21.92 | 23.29 | 24.66 | 26.03 | 27.40 | 28.77 | 30.14 | 31.51 | 32.88 | 34.25 | 35.62 | 36.99 | 38.36 | 39.73 | 41.10 |
| 74 | 21.62 | 22.97 | 24.32 | 25.68 | 27.03 | 28.38 | 29.73 | 31.08 | 32.43 | 33.78 | 35.14 | 36.49 | 37.84 | 39.19 | 40.54 |
| 75 | 21.33 | 22.67 | 24.00 | 25.33 | 26.67 | 28.00 | 29.33 | 30.67 | 32.00 | 33.33 | 34.67 | 36.00 | 37.33 | 38.67 | 40.00 |

| Total Number Correct | Number Correct on Subtest (Visual, Auditory, or Kinesthetic) | | | | | | | | | | | | | | |
|---|---|---|---|---|---|---|---|---|---|---|---|---|---|---|---|
| | 16 | 17 | 18 | 19 | 20 | 21 | 22 | 23 | 24 | 25 | 26 | 27 | 28 | 29 | 30 |
| 76 | 21.05 | 22.37 | 23.68 | 25.00 | 26.32 | 27.63 | 28.95 | 30.26 | 31.58 | 32.89 | 34.21 | 35.53 | 36.84 | 38.16 | 39.47 |
| 77 | 20.78 | 22.08 | 23.38 | 24.68 | 25.97 | 27.27 | 28.57 | 29.87 | 31.17 | 32.47 | 33.77 | 35.06 | 36.36 | 37.66 | 38.96 |
| 78 | 20.51 | 21.79 | 23.08 | 24.36 | 25.64 | 26.92 | 28.21 | 29.49 | 30.77 | 32.05 | 33.33 | 34.62 | 35.90 | 37.18 | 38.46 |
| 79 | 20.25 | 21.52 | 22.78 | 24.05 | 25.32 | 26.58 | 27.85 | 29.11 | 30.38 | 31.65 | 32.91 | 34.18 | 35.44 | 36.71 | 37.97 |
| 80 | 20.00 | 21.25 | 22.50 | 23.75 | 25.00 | 26.25 | 27.50 | 28.75 | 30.00 | 31.25 | 32.50 | 33.75 | 35.00 | 36.25 | 37.50 |
| 81 | 19.75 | 20.99 | 22.22 | 23.46 | 24.69 | 25.93 | 27.16 | 28.40 | 29.63 | 30.86 | 32.10 | 33.33 | 34.57 | 35.80 | 37.04 |
| 82 | 19.51 | 20.73 | 21.95 | 23.17 | 24.39 | 25.61 | 26.83 | 28.05 | 29.27 | 30.49 | 31.71 | 32.93 | 34.15 | 35.37 | 36.59 |
| 83 | 19.28 | 20.48 | 21.69 | 22.89 | 24.10 | 25.30 | 26.51 | 27.71 | 28.92 | 30.12 | 31.33 | 32.53 | 33.73 | 34.94 | 36.14 |
| 84 | 19.05 | 20.24 | 21.43 | 22.62 | 23.81 | 25.00 | 26.19 | 27.38 | 28.57 | 29.76 | 30.95 | 32.14 | 33.33 | 34.52 | 35.71 |
| 85 | 18.82 | 20.00 | 21.18 | 22.35 | 23.53 | 24.71 | 25.88 | 27.06 | 28.24 | 29.41 | 30.59 | 31.76 | 32.94 | 34.12 | 35.29 |
| 86 | 18.60 | 19.77 | 20.93 | 22.09 | 23.26 | 24.42 | 25.58 | 26.74 | 27.91 | 29.07 | 30.23 | 31.40 | 32.56 | 33.72 | 34.88 |
| 87 | 18.39 | 19.54 | 20.69 | 21.84 | 22.99 | 24.14 | 25.29 | 26.44 | 27.59 | 28.74 | 29.89 | 31.03 | 32.18 | 33.33 | 34.48 |
| 88 | 18.18 | 19.32 | 20.45 | 21.59 | 22.73 | 23.86 | 25.00 | 26.14 | 27.27 | 28.41 | 29.55 | 30.68 | 31.82 | 32.95 | 34.09 |
| 89 | 17.98 | 19.10 | 20.22 | 21.35 | 22.47 | 23.60 | 24.72 | 25.84 | 26.97 | 28.09 | 29.21 | 30.34 | 31.46 | 32.58 | 33.71 |
| 90 | 17.78 | 18.89 | 20.00 | 21.11 | 22.22 | 23.33 | 24.44 | 25.56 | 26.67 | 27.78 | 28.89 | 30.00 | 31.11 | 32.22 | 33.33 |
| 91 | 17.58 | 18.68 | 19.78 | 20.88 | 21.98 | 23.08 | 24.18 | 25.27 | 26.37 | 27.47 | 28.57 | 29.67 | 30.77 | 31.87 | 32.97 |
| 92 | 17.39 | 18.48 | 19.57 | 20.65 | 21.74 | 22.83 | 23.91 | 25.00 | 26.09 | 27.17 | 28.26 | 29.35 | 30.43 | 31.52 | 32.61 |
| 93 | 17.20 | 18.28 | 19.35 | 20.43 | 21.51 | 22.58 | 23.66 | 24.73 | 25.81 | 26.88 | 27.96 | 29.03 | 30.11 | 31.18 | 32.26 |
| 94 | 17.02 | 18.09 | 19.15 | 20.21 | 21.28 | 22.34 | 23.40 | 24.47 | 25.53 | 26.60 | 27.66 | 28.72 | 29.79 | 30.85 | 31.91 |
| 95 | 16.84 | 17.89 | 18.95 | 20.00 | 21.05 | 22.11 | 23.16 | 24.21 | 25.26 | 26.32 | 27.37 | 28.42 | 29.47 | 30.53 | 31.58 |
| 96 | 16.67 | 17.71 | 18.75 | 19.79 | 20.83 | 21.88 | 22.92 | 23.96 | 25.00 | 26.04 | 27.08 | 28.13 | 29.17 | 30.21 | 31.25 |
| 97 | 16.49 | 17.53 | 18.56 | 19.59 | 20.62 | 21.65 | 22.68 | 23.71 | 24.74 | 25.77 | 26.80 | 27.84 | 28.87 | 29.90 | 30.93 |
| 98 | 16.33 | 17.35 | 18.37 | 19.39 | 20.41 | 21.43 | 22.45 | 23.47 | 24.49 | 25.51 | 26.53 | 27.55 | 28.57 | 29.59 | 30.61 |
| 99 | 16.16 | 17.17 | 18.18 | 19.19 | 20.20 | 21.21 | 22.22 | 23.23 | 24.24 | 25.25 | 26.26 | 27.27 | 28.28 | 29.29 | 30.30 |
| 100 | 16.00 | 17.00 | 18.00 | 19.00 | 20.00 | 21.00 | 22.00 | 23.00 | 24.00 | 25.00 | 26.00 | 27.00 | 28.00 | 29.00 | 30.00 |
| 101 | 15.84 | 16.83 | 17.82 | 18.81 | 19.80 | 20.79 | 21.78 | 22.77 | 23.76 | 24.75 | 25.74 | 26.73 | 27.72 | 28.71 | 29.70 |
| 102 | 15.69 | 16.67 | 17.65 | 18.63 | 19.61 | 20.59 | 21.57 | 22.55 | 23.53 | 24.51 | 25.49 | 26.47 | 27.45 | 28.43 | 29.41 |
| 103 | 15.53 | 16.50 | 17.48 | 18.45 | 19.42 | 20.39 | 21.36 | 22.33 | 23.30 | 24.27 | 25.24 | 26.21 | 27.18 | 28.16 | 29.13 |
| 104 | 15.38 | 16.35 | 17.31 | 18.27 | 19.23 | 20.19 | 21.15 | 22.12 | 23.08 | 24.04 | 25.00 | 25.96 | 26.92 | 27.88 | 28.85 |
| 105 | 15.24 | 16.19 | 17.14 | 18.10 | 19.05 | 20.00 | 20.95 | 21.90 | 22.86 | 23.81 | 24.76 | 25.71 | 26.67 | 27.62 | 28.57 |
| 106 | 15.09 | 16.04 | 16.98 | 17.92 | 18.87 | 19.81 | 20.75 | 21.70 | 22.64 | 23.58 | 24.53 | 25.47 | 26.42 | 27.36 | 28.30 |
| 107 | 14.95 | 15.89 | 16.82 | 17.76 | 18.69 | 19.63 | 20.56 | 21.50 | 22.43 | 23.36 | 24.30 | 25.23 | 26.17 | 27.10 | 28.04 |
| 108 | 14.81 | 15.74 | 16.67 | 17.59 | 18.52 | 19.44 | 20.37 | 21.30 | 22.22 | 23.15 | 24.07 | 25.00 | 25.93 | 26.85 | 27.78 |
| 109 | 14.68 | 15.60 | 16.51 | 17.43 | 18.35 | 19.27 | 20.18 | 21.10 | 22.02 | 22.94 | 23.85 | 24.77 | 25.69 | 26.61 | 27.52 |
| 110 | 14.55 | 15.45 | 16.36 | 17.27 | 18.18 | 19.09 | 20.00 | 20.91 | 21.82 | 22.73 | 23.64 | 24.55 | 25.45 | 26.36 | 27.27 |
| 111 | 14.41 | 15.32 | 16.22 | 17.12 | 18.02 | 18.92 | 19.82 | 20.72 | 21.62 | 22.52 | 23.42 | 24.32 | 25.23 | 26.13 | 27.03 |
| 112 | 14.29 | 15.18 | 16.07 | 16.96 | 17.86 | 18.75 | 19.64 | 20.54 | 21.43 | 22.32 | 23.21 | 24.11 | 25.00 | 25.89 | 26.79 |
| 113 | 14.16 | 15.04 | 15.93 | 16.81 | 17.70 | 18.58 | 19.47 | 20.35 | 21.24 | 22.12 | 23.01 | 23.89 | 24.78 | 25.66 | 26.55 |
| 114 | 14.04 | 14.91 | 15.79 | 16.67 | 17.54 | 18.42 | 19.30 | 20.18 | 21.05 | 21.93 | 22.81 | 23.68 | 24.56 | 25.44 | 26.32 |
| 115 | 13.91 | 14.78 | 15.65 | 16.52 | 17.39 | 18.26 | 19.13 | 20.00 | 20.87 | 21.74 | 22.61 | 23.48 | 24.35 | 25.22 | 26.09 |
| 116 | 13.79 | 14.66 | 15.52 | 16.38 | 17.24 | 18.10 | 18.97 | 19.83 | 20.69 | 21.55 | 22.41 | 23.28 | 24.14 | 25.00 | 25.86 |
| 117 | 13.68 | 14.53 | 15.38 | 16.24 | 17.09 | 17.95 | 18.80 | 19.66 | 20.51 | 21.37 | 22.22 | 23.08 | 23.93 | 24.79 | 25.64 |
| 118 | 13.56 | 14.41 | 15.25 | 16.10 | 16.95 | 17.80 | 18.64 | 19.49 | 20.34 | 21.19 | 22.03 | 22.88 | 23.73 | 24.58 | 25.42 |
| 119 | 13.45 | 14.29 | 15.13 | 15.97 | 16.81 | 17.65 | 18.49 | 19.33 | 20.17 | 21.01 | 21.85 | 22.69 | 23.53 | 24.37 | 25.21 |
| 120 | 13.33 | 14.17 | 15.00 | 15.83 | 16.67 | 17.50 | 18.33 | 19.17 | 20.00 | 20.83 | 21.67 | 22.50 | 23.33 | 24.17 | 25.00 |
| 121 | 13.22 | 14.05 | 14.88 | 15.70 | 16.53 | 17.36 | 18.18 | 19.01 | 19.83 | 20.66 | 21.49 | 22.31 | 23.14 | 23.97 | 24.79 |
| 122 | 13.11 | 13.93 | 14.75 | 15.57 | 16.39 | 17.21 | 18.03 | 18.85 | 19.67 | 20.49 | 21.31 | 22.13 | 22.95 | 23.77 | 24.59 |
| 123 | 13.01 | 13.82 | 14.63 | 15.45 | 16.26 | 17.07 | 17.89 | 18.70 | 19.51 | 20.33 | 21.14 | 21.95 | 22.76 | 23.58 | 24.39 |
| 124 | 12.90 | 13.71 | 14.52 | 15.32 | 16.13 | 16.94 | 17.74 | 18.55 | 19.35 | 20.16 | 20.97 | 21.77 | 22.58 | 23.39 | 24.19 |
| 125 | 12.80 | 13.60 | 14.40 | 15.20 | 16.00 | 16.80 | 17.60 | 18.40 | 19.20 | 20.00 | 20.80 | 21.60 | 22.40 | 23.20 | 24.00 |
| 126 | 12.70 | 13.49 | 14.29 | 15.08 | 15.87 | 16.67 | 17.46 | 18.25 | 19.05 | 19.84 | 20.63 | 21.43 | 22.22 | 23.02 | 23.81 |
| 127 | 12.60 | 13.39 | 14.17 | 14.96 | 15.75 | 16.54 | 17.32 | 18.11 | 18.90 | 19.69 | 20.47 | 21.26 | 22.05 | 22.83 | 23.62 |
| 128 | 12.50 | 13.28 | 14.06 | 14.84 | 15.63 | 16.41 | 17.19 | 17.97 | 18.75 | 19.53 | 20.31 | 21.09 | 21.88 | 22.66 | 23.44 |
| 129 | 12.40 | 13.18 | 13.95 | 14.73 | 15.50 | 16.28 | 17.05 | 17.83 | 18.60 | 19.38 | 20.16 | 20.93 | 21.71 | 22.48 | 23.26 |
| 130 | 12.31 | 13.08 | 13.85 | 14.62 | 15.38 | 16.15 | 16.92 | 17.69 | 18.46 | 19.23 | 20.00 | 20.77 | 21.54 | 22.31 | 23.08 |
| 131 | 12.21 | 12.98 | 13.74 | 14.50 | 15.27 | 16.03 | 16.79 | 17.56 | 18.32 | 19.08 | 19.85 | 20.61 | 21.37 | 22.14 | 22.90 |
| 132 | 12.12 | 12.88 | 13.64 | 14.39 | 15.15 | 15.91 | 16.67 | 17.42 | 18.18 | 18.94 | 19.70 | 20.45 | 21.21 | 21.97 | 22.73 |
| 133 | 12.03 | 12.78 | 13.53 | 14.29 | 15.04 | 15.79 | 16.54 | 17.29 | 18.05 | 18.80 | 19.55 | 20.30 | 21.05 | 21.80 | 22.56 |
| 134 | 11.94 | 12.69 | 13.43 | 14.18 | 14.93 | 15.67 | 16.42 | 17.16 | 17.91 | 18.66 | 19.40 | 20.15 | 20.90 | 21.64 | 22.39 |
| 135 | 11.85 | 12.59 | 13.33 | 14.07 | 14.81 | 15.56 | 16.30 | 17.04 | 17.78 | 18.52 | 19.26 | 20.00 | 20.74 | 21.48 | 22.22 |

| Total Number Correct | Number Correct on Subtest (Visual, Auditory, or Kinesthetic) | | | | | | | | | | | | | | |
|---|---|---|---|---|---|---|---|---|---|---|---|---|---|---|---|
| | 31 | 32 | 33 | 34 | 35 | 36 | 37 | 38 | 39 | 40 | 41 | 42 | 43 | 44 | 45 |
| 31 | 100.00 | | | | | | | | | | | | | | |
| 32 | 96.88 | 100.00 | | | | | | | | | | | | | |
| 33 | 93.94 | 96.97 | 100.00 | | | | | | | | | | | | |
| 34 | 91.18 | 94.12 | 97.06 | 100.00 | | | | | | | | | | | |
| 35 | 88.57 | 91.43 | 94.29 | 97.14 | 100.00 | | | | | | | | | | |
| 36 | 86.11 | 88.89 | 91.67 | 94.44 | 97.22 | 100.00 | | | | | | | | | |
| 37 | 83.78 | 86.49 | 89.19 | 91.89 | 94.59 | 97.30 | 100.00 | | | | | | | | |
| 38 | 81.58 | 84.21 | 86.84 | 89.47 | 92.11 | 94.74 | 97.37 | 100.00 | | | | | | | |
| 39 | 79.49 | 82.05 | 84.62 | 87.18 | 89.74 | 92.31 | 94.87 | 97.44 | 100.00 | | | | | | |
| 40 | 77.50 | 80.00 | 82.50 | 85.00 | 87.50 | 90.00 | 92.50 | 95.00 | 97.50 | 100.00 | | | | | |
| 41 | 75.61 | 78.05 | 80.49 | 82.93 | 85.37 | 87.80 | 90.24 | 92.68 | 95.12 | 97.56 | 100.00 | | | | |
| 42 | 73.81 | 76.19 | 78.57 | 80.95 | 83.33 | 85.71 | 88.10 | 90.48 | 92.86 | 95.24 | 97.62 | 100.00 | | | |
| 43 | 72.09 | 74.42 | 76.74 | 79.07 | 81.40 | 83.72 | 86.05 | 88.37 | 90.70 | 93.02 | 95.35 | 97.67 | 100.00 | | |
| 44 | 70.45 | 72.73 | 75.00 | 77.27 | 79.55 | 81.82 | 84.09 | 86.36 | 88.64 | 90.91 | 93.18 | 95.45 | 97.73 | 100.00 | |
| 45 | 68.89 | 71.11 | 73.33 | 75.56 | 77.78 | 80.00 | 82.22 | 84.44 | 86.67 | 88.89 | 91.11 | 93.33 | 95.56 | 97.78 | 100.00 |
| 46 | 67.39 | 69.57 | 71.74 | 73.91 | 76.09 | 78.26 | 80.43 | 82.61 | 84.78 | 86.96 | 89.13 | 91.30 | 93.48 | 95.65 | 97.83 |
| 47 | 65.96 | 68.09 | 70.21 | 72.34 | 74.47 | 76.60 | 78.72 | 80.85 | 82.98 | 85.11 | 87.23 | 89.36 | 91.49 | 93.62 | 95.74 |
| 48 | 64.58 | 66.67 | 68.75 | 70.83 | 72.92 | 75.00 | 77.08 | 79.17 | 81.25 | 83.33 | 85.42 | 87.50 | 89.58 | 91.67 | 93.75 |
| 49 | 63.27 | 65.31 | 67.35 | 69.39 | 71.43 | 73.47 | 75.51 | 77.55 | 79.59 | 81.63 | 83.67 | 85.71 | 87.76 | 89.80 | 91.84 |
| 50 | 62.00 | 64.00 | 66.00 | 68.00 | 70.00 | 72.00 | 74.00 | 76.00 | 78.00 | 80.00 | 82.00 | 84.00 | 86.00 | 88.00 | 90.00 |
| 51 | 60.78 | 62.75 | 64.71 | 66.67 | 68.63 | 70.59 | 72.55 | 74.51 | 76.47 | 78.43 | 80.39 | 82.35 | 84.31 | 86.27 | 88.24 |
| 52 | 59.62 | 61.54 | 63.46 | 65.38 | 67.31 | 69.23 | 71.15 | 73.08 | 75.00 | 76.92 | 78.85 | 80.77 | 82.69 | 84.62 | 86.54 |
| 53 | 58.49 | 60.38 | 62.26 | 64.15 | 66.04 | 67.92 | 69.81 | 71.70 | 73.58 | 75.47 | 77.36 | 79.25 | 81.13 | 83.02 | 84.91 |
| 54 | 57.41 | 59.26 | 61.11 | 62.96 | 64.81 | 66.67 | 68.52 | 70.37 | 72.22 | 74.07 | 75.93 | 77.78 | 79.63 | 81.48 | 83.33 |
| 55 | 56.36 | 58.18 | 60.00 | 61.82 | 63.64 | 65.45 | 67.27 | 69.09 | 70.91 | 72.73 | 74.55 | 76.36 | 78.18 | 80.00 | 81.82 |
| 56 | 55.36 | 57.14 | 58.93 | 60.71 | 62.50 | 64.29 | 66.07 | 67.86 | 69.64 | 71.43 | 73.21 | 75.00 | 76.79 | 78.57 | 80.36 |
| 57 | 54.39 | 56.14 | 57.89 | 59.65 | 61.40 | 63.16 | 64.91 | 66.67 | 68.42 | 70.18 | 71.93 | 73.68 | 75.44 | 77.19 | 78.95 |
| 58 | 53.45 | 55.17 | 56.90 | 58.62 | 60.34 | 62.07 | 63.79 | 65.52 | 67.24 | 68.97 | 70.69 | 72.41 | 74.14 | 75.86 | 77.59 |
| 59 | 52.54 | 54.24 | 55.93 | 57.63 | 59.32 | 61.02 | 62.71 | 64.41 | 66.10 | 67.80 | 69.49 | 71.19 | 72.88 | 74.58 | 76.27 |
| 60 | 51.67 | 53.33 | 55.00 | 56.67 | 58.33 | 60.00 | 61.67 | 63.33 | 65.00 | 66.67 | 68.33 | 70.00 | 71.67 | 73.33 | 75.00 |
| 61 | 50.82 | 52.46 | 54.10 | 55.74 | 57.38 | 59.02 | 60.66 | 62.30 | 63.93 | 65.57 | 67.21 | 68.85 | 70.49 | 72.13 | 73.77 |
| 62 | 50.00 | 51.61 | 53.23 | 54.84 | 56.45 | 58.06 | 59.68 | 61.29 | 62.90 | 64.52 | 66.13 | 67.74 | 69.35 | 70.97 | 72.58 |
| 63 | 49.21 | 50.79 | 52.38 | 53.97 | 55.56 | 57.14 | 58.73 | 60.32 | 61.90 | 63.49 | 65.08 | 66.67 | 68.25 | 69.84 | 71.43 |
| 64 | 48.44 | 50.00 | 51.56 | 53.13 | 54.69 | 56.25 | 57.81 | 59.38 | 60.94 | 62.50 | 64.06 | 65.63 | 67.19 | 68.75 | 70.31 |
| 65 | 47.69 | 49.23 | 50.77 | 52.31 | 53.85 | 55.38 | 56.92 | 58.46 | 60.00 | 61.54 | 63.08 | 64.62 | 66.15 | 67.69 | 69.23 |
| 66 | 46.97 | 48.48 | 50.00 | 51.52 | 53.03 | 54.55 | 56.06 | 57.58 | 59.09 | 60.61 | 62.12 | 63.64 | 65.15 | 66.67 | 68.18 |
| 67 | 46.27 | 47.76 | 49.25 | 50.75 | 52.24 | 53.73 | 55.22 | 56.72 | 58.21 | 59.70 | 61.19 | 62.69 | 64.18 | 65.67 | 67.16 |
| 68 | 45.59 | 47.06 | 48.53 | 50.00 | 51.47 | 52.94 | 54.41 | 55.88 | 57.35 | 58.82 | 60.29 | 61.76 | 63.24 | 64.71 | 66.18 |
| 69 | 44.93 | 46.38 | 47.83 | 49.28 | 50.72 | 52.17 | 53.62 | 55.07 | 56.52 | 57.97 | 59.42 | 60.87 | 62.32 | 63.77 | 65.22 |
| 70 | 44.29 | 45.71 | 47.14 | 48.57 | 50.00 | 51.43 | 52.86 | 54.29 | 55.71 | 57.14 | 58.57 | 60.00 | 61.43 | 62.86 | 64.29 |
| 71 | 43.66 | 45.07 | 46.48 | 47.89 | 49.30 | 50.70 | 52.11 | 53.52 | 54.93 | 56.34 | 57.75 | 59.15 | 60.56 | 61.97 | 63.38 |
| 72 | 43.06 | 44.44 | 45.83 | 47.22 | 48.61 | 50.00 | 51.39 | 52.78 | 54.17 | 55.56 | 56.94 | 58.33 | 59.72 | 61.11 | 62.50 |
| 73 | 42.47 | 43.84 | 45.21 | 46.58 | 47.95 | 49.32 | 50.68 | 52.05 | 53.42 | 54.79 | 56.16 | 57.53 | 58.90 | 60.27 | 61.64 |
| 74 | 41.89 | 43.24 | 44.59 | 45.95 | 47.30 | 48.65 | 50.00 | 51.35 | 52.70 | 54.05 | 55.41 | 56.76 | 58.11 | 59.46 | 60.81 |
| 75 | 41.33 | 42.67 | 44.00 | 45.33 | 46.67 | 48.00 | 49.33 | 50.67 | 52.00 | 53.33 | 54.67 | 56.00 | 57.33 | 58.67 | 60.00 |
| 76 | 40.79 | 42.11 | 43.42 | 44.74 | 46.05 | 47.37 | 48.68 | 50.00 | 51.32 | 52.63 | 53.95 | 55.26 | 56.58 | 57.89 | 59.21 |
| 77 | 40.26 | 41.56 | 42.86 | 44.16 | 45.45 | 46.75 | 48.05 | 49.35 | 50.65 | 51.95 | 53.25 | 54.55 | 55.84 | 57.14 | 58.44 |
| 78 | 39.74 | 41.03 | 42.31 | 43.59 | 44.87 | 46.15 | 47.44 | 48.72 | 50.00 | 51.28 | 52.56 | 53.85 | 55.13 | 56.41 | 57.69 |
| 79 | 39.24 | 40.51 | 41.77 | 43.04 | 44.30 | 45.57 | 46.84 | 48.10 | 49.37 | 50.63 | 51.90 | 53.16 | 54.43 | 55.70 | 56.96 |
| 80 | 38.75 | 40.00 | 41.25 | 42.50 | 43.75 | 45.00 | 46.25 | 47.50 | 48.75 | 50.00 | 51.25 | 52.50 | 53.75 | 55.00 | 56.25 |
| 81 | 38.27 | 39.51 | 40.74 | 41.98 | 43.21 | 44.44 | 45.68 | 46.91 | 48.15 | 49.38 | 50.62 | 51.85 | 53.09 | 54.32 | 55.56 |
| 82 | 37.80 | 39.02 | 40.24 | 41.46 | 42.68 | 43.90 | 45.12 | 46.34 | 47.56 | 48.78 | 50.00 | 51.22 | 52.44 | 53.66 | 54.88 |
| 83 | 37.35 | 38.55 | 39.76 | 40.96 | 42.17 | 43.37 | 44.58 | 45.78 | 46.99 | 48.19 | 49.40 | 50.60 | 51.81 | 53.01 | 54.22 |
| 84 | 36.90 | 38.10 | 39.29 | 40.48 | 41.67 | 42.86 | 44.05 | 45.24 | 46.43 | 47.62 | 48.81 | 50.00 | 51.19 | 52.38 | 53.57 |
| 85 | 36.47 | 37.65 | 38.82 | 40.00 | 41.18 | 42.35 | 43.53 | 44.71 | 45.88 | 47.06 | 48.24 | 49.41 | 50.59 | 51.76 | 52.94 |

| Total Number Correct | Number Correct on Subtest (Visual, Auditory, or Kinesthetic) | | | | | | | | | | | | | | |
|---|---|---|---|---|---|---|---|---|---|---|---|---|---|---|---|
| | 31 | 32 | 33 | 34 | 35 | 36 | 37 | 38 | 39 | 40 | 41 | 42 | 43 | 44 | 45 |
| 86 | 36.05 | 37.21 | 38.37 | 39.53 | 40.70 | 41.86 | 43.02 | 44.19 | 45.35 | 46.51 | 47.67 | 48.84 | 50.00 | 51.16 | 52.33 |
| 87 | 35.63 | 36.78 | 37.93 | 39.08 | 40.23 | 41.38 | 42.53 | 43.68 | 44.83 | 45.98 | 47.13 | 48.28 | 49.43 | 50.57 | 51.72 |
| 88 | 35.23 | 36.36 | 37.50 | 38.64 | 39.77 | 40.91 | 42.05 | 43.18 | 44.32 | 45.45 | 46.59 | 47.73 | 48.86 | 50.00 | 51.14 |
| 89 | 34.83 | 35.96 | 37.08 | 38.20 | 39.33 | 40.45 | 41.57 | 42.70 | 43.82 | 44.94 | 46.07 | 47.19 | 48.31 | 49.44 | 50.56 |
| 90 | 34.44 | 35.56 | 36.67 | 37.78 | 38.89 | 40.00 | 41.11 | 42.22 | 43.33 | 44.44 | 45.56 | 46.67 | 47.78 | 48.89 | 50.00 |
| 91 | 34.07 | 35.16 | 36.26 | 37.36 | 38.46 | 39.56 | 40.66 | 41.76 | 42.86 | 43.96 | 45.05 | 46.15 | 47.25 | 48.35 | 49.45 |
| 92 | 33.70 | 34.78 | 35.87 | 36.96 | 38.04 | 39.13 | 40.22 | 41.30 | 42.39 | 43.48 | 44.57 | 45.65 | 46.74 | 47.83 | 48.91 |
| 93 | 33.33 | 34.41 | 35.48 | 36.56 | 37.63 | 38.71 | 39.78 | 40.86 | 41.94 | 43.01 | 44.09 | 45.16 | 46.24 | 47.31 | 48.39 |
| 94 | 32.98 | 34.04 | 35.11 | 36.17 | 37.23 | 38.30 | 39.36 | 40.43 | 41.49 | 42.55 | 43.62 | 44.68 | 45.74 | 46.81 | 47.87 |
| 95 | 32.63 | 33.68 | 34.74 | 35.79 | 36.84 | 37.89 | 38.95 | 40.00 | 41.05 | 42.11 | 43.16 | 44.21 | 45.26 | 46.32 | 47.37 |
| 96 | 32.29 | 33.33 | 34.38 | 35.42 | 36.46 | 37.50 | 38.54 | 39.58 | 40.63 | 41.67 | 42.71 | 43.75 | 44.79 | 45.83 | 46.88 |
| 97 | 31.96 | 32.99 | 34.02 | 35.05 | 36.08 | 37.11 | 38.14 | 39.18 | 40.21 | 41.24 | 42.27 | 43.30 | 44.33 | 45.36 | 46.39 |
| 98 | 31.63 | 32.65 | 33.67 | 34.69 | 35.71 | 36.73 | 37.76 | 38.78 | 39.80 | 40.82 | 41.84 | 42.86 | 43.88 | 44.90 | 45.92 |
| 99 | 31.31 | 32.32 | 33.33 | 34.34 | 35.35 | 36.36 | 37.37 | 38.38 | 39.39 | 40.40 | 41.41 | 42.42 | 43.43 | 44.44 | 45.45 |
| 100 | 31.00 | 32.00 | 33.00 | 34.00 | 35.00 | 36.00 | 37.00 | 38.00 | 39.00 | 40.00 | 41.00 | 42.00 | 43.00 | 44.00 | 45.00 |
| 101 | 30.69 | 31.68 | 32.67 | 33.66 | 34.65 | 35.64 | 36.63 | 37.62 | 38.61 | 39.60 | 40.59 | 41.58 | 42.57 | 43.56 | 44.55 |
| 102 | 30.39 | 31.37 | 32.35 | 33.33 | 34.31 | 35.29 | 36.27 | 37.25 | 38.24 | 39.22 | 40.20 | 41.18 | 42.16 | 43.14 | 44.12 |
| 103 | 30.10 | 31.07 | 32.04 | 33.01 | 33.98 | 34.95 | 35.92 | 36.89 | 37.86 | 38.83 | 39.81 | 40.78 | 41.75 | 42.72 | 43.69 |
| 104 | 29.81 | 30.77 | 31.73 | 32.69 | 33.65 | 34.62 | 35.58 | 36.54 | 37.50 | 38.46 | 39.42 | 40.38 | 41.35 | 42.31 | 43.27 |
| 105 | 29.52 | 30.48 | 31.43 | 32.38 | 33.33 | 34.29 | 35.24 | 36.19 | 37.14 | 38.10 | 39.05 | 40.00 | 40.95 | 41.90 | 42.86 |
| 106 | 29.25 | 30.19 | 31.13 | 32.08 | 33.02 | 33.96 | 34.91 | 35.85 | 36.79 | 37.74 | 38.68 | 39.62 | 40.57 | 41.51 | 42.45 |
| 107 | 28.97 | 29.91 | 30.84 | 31.78 | 32.71 | 33.64 | 34.58 | 35.51 | 36.45 | 37.38 | 38.32 | 39.25 | 40.19 | 41.12 | 42.06 |
| 108 | 28.70 | 29.63 | 30.56 | 31.48 | 32.41 | 33.33 | 34.26 | 35.19 | 36.11 | 37.04 | 37.96 | 38.89 | 39.81 | 40.74 | 41.67 |
| 109 | 28.44 | 29.36 | 30.28 | 31.19 | 32.11 | 33.03 | 33.94 | 34.86 | 35.78 | 36.70 | 37.61 | 38.53 | 39.45 | 40.37 | 41.28 |
| 110 | 28.18 | 29.09 | 30.00 | 30.91 | 31.82 | 32.73 | 33.64 | 34.55 | 35.45 | 36.36 | 37.27 | 38.18 | 39.09 | 40.00 | 40.91 |
| 111 | 27.93 | 28.83 | 29.73 | 30.63 | 31.53 | 32.43 | 33.33 | 34.23 | 35.14 | 36.04 | 36.94 | 37.84 | 38.74 | 39.64 | 40.54 |
| 112 | 27.68 | 28.57 | 29.46 | 30.36 | 31.25 | 32.14 | 33.04 | 33.93 | 34.82 | 35.71 | 36.61 | 37.50 | 38.39 | 39.29 | 40.18 |
| 113 | 27.43 | 28.32 | 29.20 | 30.09 | 30.97 | 31.86 | 32.74 | 33.63 | 34.51 | 35.40 | 36.28 | 37.17 | 38.05 | 38.94 | 39.82 |
| 114 | 27.19 | 28.07 | 28.95 | 29.82 | 30.70 | 31.58 | 32.46 | 33.33 | 34.21 | 35.09 | 35.96 | 36.84 | 37.72 | 38.60 | 39.47 |
| 115 | 26.96 | 27.83 | 28.70 | 29.57 | 30.43 | 31.30 | 32.17 | 33.04 | 33.91 | 34.78 | 35.65 | 36.52 | 37.39 | 38.26 | 39.13 |
| 116 | 26.72 | 27.59 | 28.45 | 29.31 | 30.17 | 31.03 | 31.90 | 32.76 | 33.62 | 34.48 | 35.34 | 36.21 | 37.07 | 37.93 | 38.79 |
| 117 | 26.50 | 27.35 | 28.21 | 29.06 | 29.91 | 30.77 | 31.62 | 32.48 | 33.33 | 34.19 | 35.04 | 35.90 | 36.75 | 37.61 | 38.46 |
| 118 | 26.27 | 27.12 | 27.97 | 28.81 | 29.66 | 30.51 | 31.36 | 32.20 | 33.05 | 33.90 | 34.75 | 35.59 | 36.44 | 37.29 | 38.14 |
| 119 | 26.05 | 26.89 | 27.73 | 28.57 | 29.41 | 30.25 | 31.09 | 31.93 | 32.77 | 33.61 | 34.45 | 35.29 | 36.13 | 36.97 | 37.82 |
| 120 | 25.83 | 26.67 | 27.50 | 28.33 | 29.17 | 30.00 | 30.83 | 31.67 | 32.50 | 33.33 | 34.17 | 35.00 | 35.83 | 36.67 | 37.50 |
| 121 | 25.62 | 26.45 | 27.27 | 28.10 | 28.93 | 29.75 | 30.58 | 31.40 | 32.23 | 33.06 | 33.88 | 34.51 | 35.54 | 36.36 | 37.19 |
| 122 | 25.41 | 26.23 | 27.05 | 27.87 | 28.69 | 29.51 | 30.33 | 31.15 | 31.97 | 32.79 | 33.61 | 34.43 | 35.25 | 36.07 | 36.89 |
| 123 | 25.20 | 26.02 | 26.83 | 27.64 | 28.46 | 29.27 | 30.08 | 30.89 | 31.71 | 32.52 | 33.33 | 34.15 | 34.96 | 35.77 | 36.59 |
| 124 | 25.00 | 25.81 | 26.61 | 27.42 | 28.23 | 29.03 | 29.84 | 30.65 | 31.45 | 32.26 | 33.06 | 33.87 | 34.68 | 35.48 | 36.29 |
| 125 | 24.80 | 25.60 | 26.40 | 27.20 | 28.00 | 28.80 | 29.60 | 30.40 | 31.20 | 32.00 | 32.80 | 33.60 | 34.40 | 35.20 | 36.00 |
| 126 | 24.60 | 25.40 | 26.19 | 26.98 | 27.78 | 28.57 | 29.37 | 30.16 | 30.95 | 31.75 | 32.54 | 33.33 | 34.13 | 34.92 | 35.71 |
| 127 | 24.41 | 25.20 | 25.98 | 26.77 | 27.56 | 28.35 | 29.13 | 29.92 | 30.71 | 31.50 | 32.28 | 33.07 | 33.86 | 34.65 | 35.43 |
| 128 | 24.22 | 25.00 | 25.78 | 26.56 | 27.34 | 28.13 | 28.91 | 29.69 | 30.47 | 31.25 | 32.03 | 32.81 | 33.59 | 34.38 | 35.16 |
| 129 | 24.03 | 24.81 | 25.58 | 26.36 | 27.13 | 27.91 | 28.68 | 29.46 | 30.23 | 31.01 | 31.78 | 32.56 | 33.33 | 34.11 | 34.88 |
| 130 | 23.85 | 24.62 | 25.38 | 26.15 | 26.92 | 27.69 | 28.46 | 29.23 | 30.00 | 30.77 | 31.54 | 32.31 | 33.08 | 33.85 | 34.62 |
| 131 | 23.66 | 24.43 | 25.19 | 25.95 | 26.72 | 27.48 | 28.24 | 29.01 | 29.77 | 30.53 | 31.30 | 32.06 | 32.82 | 33.59 | 34.35 |
| 132 | 23.48 | 24.24 | 25.00 | 25.76 | 26.52 | 27.27 | 28.03 | 28.79 | 29.55 | 30.30 | 31.06 | 31.82 | 32.58 | 33.33 | 34.09 |
| 133 | 23.31 | 24.06 | 24.81 | 25.56 | 26.32 | 27.07 | 27.82 | 28.57 | 29.32 | 30.08 | 30.83 | 31.58 | 32.33 | 33.08 | 33.83 |
| 134 | 23.13 | 23.88 | 24.63 | 25.37 | 26.12 | 26.87 | 27.61 | 28.36 | 29.10 | 29.85 | 30.60 | 31.34 | 32.09 | 32.84 | 33.58 |
| 135 | 22.96 | 23.70 | 24.44 | 25.19 | 25.93 | 26.67 | 27.41 | 28.15 | 28.89 | 29.63 | 30.37 | 31.11 | 31.85 | 32.59 | 33.33 |

# Standardization of the SBMI: Technical Report

The psychometric properties of the Swassing-Barbe Modality Index and changes in modality scores that are a function of sex, handedness, and grade were discussed briefly in Chapter IV. This Appendix extends the discussion by presenting the statistics associated with the standardization of the SBMI. The contents of this section are technical, and are intended for researchers and educational practitioners who have an interest in and an understanding of data analysis.

*Sample.* The data summarized in this Appendix were obtained from 637 students in grades kindergarten through six in a large southern California elementary school district. Of this sample, 45.9 percent were female, and 54.1 percent were male; 11.5 percent of the entire group were left-handed. Grade breakdowns for the sample are provided in several of the tables. Approximately 30 percent of the students in the sample were of Hispanic origin. The district comprises urban, suburban, and semi-rural areas.

The over-representation of Hispanic students caused some concern. If these students evidenced modality scores that differed significantly from the remainder of the students in the sample, then the generalizability of the results of the standardization research would be limited. An analysis of variance showed that within each grade, the modality raw scores and percentage scores of Hispanic students did not differ significantly from those of their peers. Further, there did not appear to be any systematic variation in the scores of the Hispanic students that was not statistically significant but would bias the results of the research. We concluded, therefore, that the large number of Hispanic students did not seriously affect the results of the study.

*Data analysis.* As was mentioned in Chapter IV, this data analysis was conducted using statistical packages. For the majority of the analyses, the *Statistical Package for the Social Sciences* (Nie, et al, 1975) was utilized. The *Biomedical Computer Programs* (Dixon, 1977) were used for analysis of variance. Unequal cell frequencies were treated as being representative of population proportions.

Supplemental Table 1   FACTOR ANALYSIS OF MODALITY RAW SCORES

| | Initial Solution | | |
| --- | --- | --- | --- |
| | Factor 1 | Factor 2 | Factor 3 |
| Visual raw scores | .84 | − .38 | .38 |
| Auditory raw scores | .78 | .61 | .13 |
| Kinesthetic raw scores | .87 | − .13 | − .49 |
| Total raw scores | .99 | − .04 | − .01 |
| Eigenvalue | 3.08 | .53 | .39 |
| Percent of variance | 76.9 | 13.3 | 9.8 |
| | Varimax Rotated Solution | | |
| Visual raw scores | .93 | .29 | .21 |
| Auditory raw scores | .22 | .25 | .94 |
| Kinesthetic raw scores | .30 | .92 | .25 |
| Total raw scores | .61 | .62 | .49 |

Supplemental Table 2   FACTOR ANALYSIS OF MODALITY RAW SCORES AND ACHIEVEMENT

| | Initial Solution | |
| --- | --- | --- |
| | Factor 1 | Factor 2 |
| Visual raw scores | .51 | .63 |
| Auditory raw scores | .61 | .38 |
| Kinesthetic raw scores | .65 | .54 |
| Total raw scores | .74 | .67 |
| Reading achievement | .81 | − .43 |
| Language achievement | .77 | − .49 |
| Math achievement | .80 | − .37 |
| Total achievement | .89 | − .43 |
| Eigenvalue | 4.27 | 2.02 |
| Percent of variance | 53.4 | 25.3 |
| | Varimax Rotated Solution | |
| Visual raw scores | .01 | .81 |
| Auditory raw scores | .24 | .67 |
| Kinesthetic raw scores | .19 | .83 |
| Total raw scores | .17 | .98 |
| Reading achievement | .90 | .16 |
| Language achievement | .91 | .09 |
| Math achievement | .85 | .20 |
| Total achievement | .97 | .20 |

*Validity.* The construct and indirect validity of the SBMI were assessed through factor analyses. The correlation matrix upon which the factor analyses were based is reported in Supplemental Table 5. The factor analyses themselves are summarized in Supplemental Tables 1 and 2. The initial solution was principal components, with the value of 1.0 occupying the main diagonal entries. The final solution was accomplished through a varimax rotation.

*Reliability.* The Guttman scale characteristics of the SBMI can be found in Supplemental Table 3. The reader who is familiar with Guttman scaling will immediately note that the coefficient of scalability for each subtest, the most important statistic in the table, is marginally acceptable. We examined the characteristics of each item on the subtests, and found that the first two and last two items were the weakest and were responsible for the marginal coefficients of scalability. The first two items were correctly completed by each subject, so they contributed little to the consistency of the scale. The last two items, if they were to be answered correctly, probably involved long term rather than short term memory. Subjects' responses on these final items were therefore inconsistent with responses to the other items which reflected short term memory only.

**Supplemental Table 3   GUTTMAN SCALE CHARACTERISTICS OF THE SBMI**

|  | Visual | Auditory | Kinesthetic |
|---|---|---|---|
| Coefficient of reproducibility | .92 | .95 | .94 |
| Minimal marginal reproducibility | .83 | .88 | .84 |
| Percent improvement | .09 | .07 | .10 |
| Coefficient of scalability | .55 | .60 | .61 |

Test-retest statistics are summarized in Supplemental Table 4. Again, these statistics fall just within the acceptable range, but compare favorably with the stability coefficients reported by Kirk, et al (1968) for the ITPA.

Supplemental Table 4 TEST-RETEST STATISTICS FOR MODALITY RAW SCORES*

|  |  | Mean | SD | Correlation |
|---|---|---|---|---|
| Visual | Test 1 | 21.04 | 11.73 | .61 |
|  | Test 2 | 26.83 | 13.10 | |
| Auditory | Test 1 | 18.47 | 11.07 | .65 |
|  | Test 2 | 21.13 | 10.37 | |
| Kinesthetic | Test 1 | 17.81 | 10.88 | .67 |
|  | Test 2 | 23.96 | 13.36 | |
| Total | Test 1 | 57.32 | 25.16 | .58 |
|  | Test 2 | 71.92 | 25.27 | |

* N = 68

*Correlational analysis.* Supplemental Tables 5 through 12 report the correlation coefficients among modality raw scores, percentages, and achievement scores. Achievement was measured as the national percentage equivalent of each student's raw score on the Comprehensive Test of Basic Skills (McGraw-Hill, 1975). A glance at the tables shows that the relationships among the variables that constitute the tables are inconsistent from year to year. Despite this inconsistency, it appears that modality raw scores correlate moderately well with achievement, and that there is almost no relationship among modality percentage scores and achievement. The former conclusion is consistent with our belief that raw scores are a rough index of cognitive development.

**Supplemental Table 5  INTERCORRELATION MATRIX AMONG MODALITY RAW SCORES, MODALITY PERCENTAGES, AND ACHIEVEMENT FOR THE ENTIRE SAMPLE**

|  | V1 | V2 | V3 | V4 | V5 | V6 | V7 | V8 | V9 | V10 | V11 |
|---|---|---|---|---|---|---|---|---|---|---|---|
| V1 | 1.00 | .48* | .60* | .85* | .53* | −.55* | −.02 | .30* | .12 | .23* | .21* |
| V2 |  | 1.00 | .54* | .76* | −.23* | .25* | −.01 | .30* | .27* | .26* | .34* |
| V3 |  |  | 1.00 | .88* | −.17* | −.46* | .65* | .29* | .23* | .24* | .34* |
| V4 |  |  |  | 1.00 | .08 | −.37* | .28* | .36* | .25* | .29* | .37* |
| V5 |  |  |  |  | 1.00 | −.53* | −.54* | .00 | −.14 | −.01 | −.11 |
| V6 |  |  |  |  |  | 1.00 | −.43* | −.13 | .03 | −.08 | −.05 |
| V7 |  |  |  |  |  |  | 1.00 | .12 | .12 | .09 | .17 |
| N of Subjects | 637 | 637 | 637 | 637 | 637 | 637 | 637 | 435 | 223 | 428 | 214 |

**Supplemental Table 6  INTERCORRELATION MATRIX AMONG MODALITY RAW SCORES, MODALITY PERCENTAGES, AND ACHIEVEMENT FOR KINDERGARTEN**

|  | V1 | V2 | V3 | V4 | V5 | V6 | V7 | V8 | V9 | V10 | V11 |
|---|---|---|---|---|---|---|---|---|---|---|---|
| V1 | 1.00 | .58* | .55* | .87* | .53* | −.31 | −.23 |  |  |  |  |
| V2 |  | 1.00 | .42* | .82* | −.15 | .45* | −.28 |  |  |  |  |
| V3 |  |  | 1.00 | .78* | −.20 | −.38 | .56* |  |  |  |  |
| V4 |  |  |  | 1.00 | .09 | −.09 | −.01 |  |  |  |  |
| V5 |  |  |  |  | 1.00 | −.48* | −.53* |  |  |  |  |
| V6 |  |  |  |  |  | 1.00 | −.49* |  |  |  |  |
| V7 |  |  |  |  |  |  | 1.00 |  |  |  |  |
| N of Subjects | 81 | 81 | 81 | 81 | 81 | 81 | 81 |  |  |  |  |

**Supplemental Table 7  INTERCORRELATION MATRIX AMONG MODALITY RAW SCORES, MODALITY PERCENTAGES, AND ACHIEVEMENT FOR FIRST GRADE**

|  | V1 | V2 | V3 | V4 | V5 | V6 | V7 | V8 | V9 | V10 | V11 |
|---|---|---|---|---|---|---|---|---|---|---|---|
| V1 | 1.00 | .27 | .23 | .74* | .65* | −.39* | −.40* | .26 | .41 | .20 | .03 |
| V2 |  | 1.00 | .39* | .73* | −.32* | .60* | −.19 | .19 | .64 | .22 | .23 |
| V3 |  |  | 1.00 | .71* | −.35* | −.20 | .61* | .13 | .54 | .26 | .43 |
| V4 |  |  |  | 1.00 | .06 | −.04 | −.03 | .27 | .68* | .32 | .29 |
| V5 |  |  |  |  | 1.00 | −.58* | −.64* | .08 | −.01 | .07 | −.30 |
| V6 |  |  |  |  |  | 1.00 | −.26 | −.03 | −.06 | −.06 | −.18 |
| V7 |  |  |  |  |  |  | 1.00 | −.06 | .07 | −.02 | .47 |
| N of Subjects | 100 | 100 | 100 | 100 | 100 | 100 | 100 | 72 | 17 | 61 | 10 |

\* Probability less than or equal to .001. Given the large number of correlation coefficients, this probability level was chosen in order to avoid inflating alpha through multiple comparisons.

| | |
|---|---|
| V1 Visual raw scores | V5 Visual percentage | V9 Language achievement |
| V2 Auditory raw scores | V6 Auditory percentage | V10 Math achievement |
| V3 Kinesthetic raw scores | V7 Kinesthetic percentage | V11 Total achievement |
| V4 Total raw scores | V8 Reading achievement | |

**89**

**Supplemental Table 8   INTERCORRELATION MATRIX AMONG MODALITY RAW SCORES, MODALITY PERCENTAGES, AND ACHIEVEMENT FOR SECOND GRADE**

|  | V1 | V2 | V3 | V4 | V5 | V6 | V7 | V8 | V9 | V10 | V11 |
|---|---|---|---|---|---|---|---|---|---|---|---|
| V1 | 1.00 | .17 | .41* | .75* | .63* | .65* | −.01 | .31 |  | .17 |  |
| V2 |  | 1.00 | .27 | .55* | −.40* | .46* | −.06 | .09 |  | .17 |  |
| V3 |  |  | 1.00 | .84* | −.18 | −.45* | .72* | .19 |  | .03 |  |
| V4 |  |  |  | 1.00 | .07 | −.41* | .39* | .28 |  | .14 |  |
| V5 |  |  |  |  | 1.00 | −.62* | −.46* | .09 |  | .06 |  |
| V6 |  |  |  |  |  | 1.00 | −.41* | −.29 |  | −.11 |  |
| V7 |  |  |  |  |  |  | 1.00 | .21 |  | .05 |  |
| N of Subjects | 118 | 118 | 118 | 118 | 118 | 118 | 118 | 85 |  | 96 |  |

**Supplemental Table 9   INTERCORRELATION MATRIX AMONG MODALITY RAW SCORES, MODALITY PERCENTAGES, AND ACHIEVEMENT FOR THIRD GRADE**

|  | V1 | V2 | V3 | V4 | V5 | V6 | V7 | V8 | V9 | V10 | V11 |
|---|---|---|---|---|---|---|---|---|---|---|---|
| V1 | 1.00 | .31 | .39* | .79* | .63* | −.47* | −.22 | .43* |  | .33 |  |
| V2 |  | 1.00 | .29 | .64* | −.27 | .53* | −.20 | .36 |  | .33 |  |
| V3 |  |  | 1.00 | .79* | −.32* | −.46* | .73* | .35 |  | .30 |  |
| V4 |  |  |  | 1.00 | .06 | −.28 | .19 | .52* |  | .43* |  |
| V5 |  |  |  |  | 1.00 | −.46* | −.61* | .09 |  | .03 |  |
| V6 |  |  |  |  |  | 1.00 | −.43* | .10 |  | −.06 |  |
| V7 |  |  |  |  |  |  | 1.00 | −.01 |  | .02 |  |
| N of Subjects | 85 | 85 | 85 | 85 | 85 | 85 | 85 | 64 |  | 59 |  |

**Supplemental Table 10   INTERCORRELATION MATRIX AMONG MODALITY RAW SCORES, MODALITY PERCENTAGES, AND ACHIEVEMENT FOR FOURTH GRADE**

|  | V1 | V2 | V3 | V4 | V5 | V6 | V7 | V8 | V9 | V10 | V11 |
|---|---|---|---|---|---|---|---|---|---|---|---|
| V1 | 1.00 | .39* | .58* | .84* | .56* | −.61* | .05 | .23 | .26 | .21 | .23 |
| V2 |  | 1.00 | .49* | .69* | −.29 | .26 | .02 | .32* | .30 | .28 | .29 |
| V3 |  |  | 1.00 | .89* | −.23 | −.57* | .75* | .38* | .33* | .37* | .42* |
| V4 |  |  |  | 1.00 | .05 | −.48* | .39* | .38* | .36* | .36* | .39* |
| V5 |  |  |  |  | 1.00 | −.42* | −.54* | −.17 | −.07 | −.16 | −.16 |
| V6 |  |  |  |  |  | 1.00 | −.54* | −.09 | −.09 | −.09 | −.12 |
| V7 |  |  |  |  |  |  | 1.00 | .23 | .14 | .21 | .25 |
| N of Subjects | 99 | 99 | 99 | 99 | 99 | 99 | 99 | 88 | 82 | 86 | 79 |

* Probability less than or equal to .001. Given the large number of correlation coefficients, this probability level was chosen in order to avoid inflating alpha through multiple comparisons.

| | | |
|---|---|---|
| V1 Visual raw scores | V5 Visual percentage | V9 Language achievement |
| V2 Auditory raw scores | V6 Auditory percentage | V10 Math achievement |
| V3 Kinesthetic raw scores | V7 Kinesthetic percentage | V11 Total achievement |
| V4 Total raw scores | V8 Reading achievement | |

Supplemental Table 11   INTERCORRELATION MATRIX AMONG MODALITY RAW SCORES, MODALITY PERCENTAGES, AND ACHIEVEMENT FOR FIFTH GRADE

|  | V1 | V2 | V3 | V4 | V5 | V6 | V7 | V8 | V9 | V10 | V11 |
|---|---|---|---|---|---|---|---|---|---|---|---|
| V1 | 1.00 | .19 | .31* | .66* | .50* | −.47* | −.16 | .03 | .10 | .29 | .15 |
| V2 |  | 1.00 | .47* | .70* | −.53* | .59* | .10 | .32* | .23 | .34* | .35* |
| V3 |  |  | 1.00 | .85* | −.57* | −.27 | .82* | .26 | .20 | .32* | .29 |
| V4 |  |  |  | 1.00 | −.29 | −.13 | .41* | .28 | .24 | .43* | .35* |
| V5 |  |  |  |  | 1.00 | −.44* | −.71* | −.29 | −.14 | −.12 | −.21 |
| V6 |  |  |  |  |  | 1.00 | −.31* | .17 | .08 | .03 | .12 |
| V7 |  |  |  |  |  |  | 1.00 | .17 | .09 | .10 | .13 |
| N of Subjects | 92 | 92 | 92 | 92 | 92 | 92 | 92 | 84 | 83 | 83 | 83 |

Supplemental Table 12   INTERCORRELATION MATRIX AMONG MODALITY RAW SCORES, MODALITY PERCENTAGES, AND ACHIEVEMENT FOR SIXTH GRADE

|  | V1 | V2 | V3 | V4 | V5 | V6 | V7 | V8 | V9 | V10 | V11 |
|---|---|---|---|---|---|---|---|---|---|---|---|
| V1 | 1.00 | .13 | .43* | .77* | .68* | −.58* | −.10 | .15 | .10 | −.04 | .05 |
| V2 |  | 1.00 | .25 | .55* | −.37* | .53* | −.15 | .32 | .44 | .26 | .38 |
| V3 |  |  | 1.00 | .82* | −.25 | −.53* | .77* | .22 | .29 | .21 | .25 |
| V4 |  |  |  | 1.00 | .08 | −.38* | .30 | .30 | .35 | .18 | .29 |
| V5 |  |  |  |  | 1.00 | −.49* | −.51* | −.12 | −.26 | −.27 | −.26 |
| V6 |  |  |  |  |  | 1.00 | −.50* | .03 | .10 | .10 | .11 |
| V7 |  |  |  |  |  |  | 1.00 | .08 | .15 | .16 | .15 |
| N of Subjects | 62 | 62 | 62 | 62 | 62 | 62 | 62 | 40 | 38 | 39 | 38 |

* Probability less than or equal to .001. Given the large number of correlation coefficients, this probability level was chosen in order to avoid inflating alpha through multiple comparisons.

| | | |
|---|---|---|
| V1 Visual raw scores | V5 Visual percentage | V9 Language achievement |
| V2 Auditory raw scores | V6 Auditory percentage | V10 Math achievement |
| V3 Kinesthetic raw scores | V7 Kinesthetic percentage | V11 Total achievement |
| V4 Total raw scores | V8 Reading achievement | |

*Relationship between modality scores and sex, handedness, and grade.* The analyses of variance reported in Supplemental Tables 13 and 14 examine the influence of sex and grade on modality raw scores and percentages. In all cases but one, the two way interaction of sex and grade is non-significant, implying that within each grade, sex has no bearing on modality raw scores and percentages. In the single instance in which a significant *F-ratio* emerged, a Scheffe follow-up test confirmed that the within-grade comparison was not the source of significance.

**Supplemental Table 13** *ANOVA* TABLE SUMMARIZING THE EFFECT OF GRADE AND SEX ON MODALITY RAW SCORES

| Source | Degrees of Freedom | Mean Square | F-ratio | Probability |
|--------|--------|--------|--------|--------|
| Visual raw score | | | | |
| Mean | 1 | 234326.93 | 3397.37 | .001 |
| Sex | 1 | 907.10 | 13.15 | .001 |
| Grade | 6 | 4241.13 | 61.49 | .001 |
| Sex by Grade | 6 | 55.88 | 0.81 | NS |
| Error | 621 | 68.97 | | |
| Auditory raw score | | | | |
| Mean | 1 | 178452.72 | 4631.63 | .001 |
| Sex | 1 | 554.45 | 14.39 | .001 |
| Grade | 6 | 1568.91 | 40.72 | .001 |
| Sex by Grade | 6 | 32.99 | 0.86 | NS |
| Error | 621 | 38.53 | | |
| Kinesthetic raw score | | | | |
| Mean | 1 | 172241.23 | 2078.90 | .001 |
| Sex | 1 | 387.73 | 4.68 | .05 |
| Grade | 6 | 3773.63 | 45.55 | .001 |
| Sex by Grade | 6 | 138.26 | 1.67 | NS |
| Error | 621 | 82.85 | | |
| Total raw score | | | | |
| Mean | 1 | 1746440.20 | 5557.09 | .001 |
| Sex | 1 | 5381.07 | 17.12 | .001 |
| Grade | 6 | 27203.40 | 86.56 | .001 |
| Sex by Grade | 6 | 283.47 | 0.90 | NS |
| Error | 621 | 314.27 | | |

It should be added that the main effect for sex proved significant in the analysis of modality raw scores, with females evidencing higher mean raw scores when grade was not a consideration. Further, within most grades, the females had higher raw scores; the male-female difference failed, however, to reach an accepted level of statistical significance. When considered together, these two findings suggest that females develop more rapidly than males in the cognitive/perceptual skills that underlie the SBMI.

**Supplemental Table 14** *ANOVA* **TABLE SUMMARIZING THE EFFECT OF GRADE AND SEX ON MODALITY PERCENTAGES**

| Source | Degrees of Freedom | Mean Square | F-ratio | Probability |
|--------|--------------------|-------------|---------|-------------|
| Visual percentage | | | | |
| Mean | 1 | 794358.52 | 6530.20 | .001 |
| Sex | 1 | 34.85 | 0.29 | NS |
| Grade | 6 | 468.51 | 3.85 | .001 |
| Sex by Grade | 6 | 201.78 | 1.66 | NS |
| Error | 621 | 121.64 | | |
| Auditory percentage | | | | |
| Mean | 1 | 690367.49 | 7022.66 | .001 |
| Sex | 1 | 7.05 | 0.07 | NS |
| Grade | 6 | 1268.37 | 12.90 | .001 |
| Sex by Grade | 6 | 110.37 | 1.12 | NS |
| Error | 621 | 98.31 | | |
| Kinesthetic percentage | | | | |
| Mean | 1 | 546701.08 | 5197.66 | .001 |
| Sex | 1 | 10.48 | 0.10 | NS |
| Grade | 6 | 367.87 | 3.50 | .01 |
| Sex by Grade | 6 | 322.22 | 3.06 | .01 |
| Error | 621 | 105.18 | | |

The effect of handedness and grade on modality raw scores and percentages was tested through the analyses of variance reported in Supplemental Tables 15 and 16. Not once did the interaction of grade and handedness prove significant. Given this finding, and the non-significant main effect for handedness, it is clear that cerebral dominance has little impact on modality strengths.

**Supplemental Table 15** *ANOVA* TABLE SUMMARIZING THE EFFECT OF GRADE AND HANDEDNESS ON MODALITY RAW SCORES

| Source | Degrees of Freedom | Mean Square | F-ratio | Probability |
|---|---|---|---|---|
| Visual raw scores | | | | |
| Mean | 1 | 91454.52 | 1287.46 | .001 |
| Handedness | 1 | 0.05 | 0.01 | NS |
| Grade | 6 | 2087.61 | 29.39 | .001 |
| Handedness by Grade | 6 | 40.88 | 0.57 | NS |
| Error | 614 | 71.03 | | |
| Auditory raw scores | | | | |
| Mean | 1 | 67956.16 | 1715.79 | .001 |
| Handedness | 1 | 22.17 | 0.56 | NS |
| Grade | 6 | 743.77 | 18.78 | .001 |
| Handedness by Grade | 6 | 31.20 | 0.79 | NS |
| Error | 614 | 39.61 | | |
| Kinesthetic raw scores | | | | |
| Mean | 1 | 65068.21 | 766.00 | .001 |
| Handedness | 1 | 49.63 | 0.58 | NS |
| Grade | 6 | 1574.46 | 18.53 | .001 |
| Handedness by Grade | 6 | 43.27 | 0.51 | NS |
| Error | 614 | 84.95 | | |
| Total raw scores | | | | |
| Mean | 1 | 669423.74 | 2052.45 | .001 |
| Handedness | 1 | 143.71 | 0.44 | NS |
| Grade | 6 | 12480.15 | 38.26 | .001 |
| Handedness by Grade | 6 | 75.43 | 0.23 | NS |
| Error | 614 | 326.16 | | |

**Supplemental Table 16** *ANOVA* TABLE SUMMARIZING THE EFFECT OF GRADE AND HANDEDNESS ON MODALITY PERCENTAGES

| Source | Degrees of Freedom | Mean Square | F-ratio | Probability |
|---|---|---|---|---|
| Visual percentage | | | | |
| Mean | 1 | 328676.95 | 2651.72 | .001 |
| Handedness | 1 | 313.37 | 2.53 | NS |
| Grade | 6 | 206.37 | 1.67 | NS |
| Handedness by Grade | 6 | 34.57 | 0.28 | NS |
| Error | 614 | 123.95 | | |
| Auditory percentage | | | | |
| Mean | 1 | 270617.79 | 2724.68 | .001 |
| Handedness | 1 | 17.46 | 0.18 | NS |
| Grade | 6 | 543.46 | 5.47 | .001 |
| Handedness by Grade | 6 | 76.39 | 0.77 | NS |
| Error | 614 | 99.32 | | |
| Kinesthetic percentage | | | | |
| Mean | 1 | 207328.28 | 1924.83 | .001 |
| Handedness | 1 | 182.88 | 1.70 | NS |
| Grade | 6 | 140.54 | 1.30 | NS |
| Handedness by Grade | 6 | 91.50 | .85 | NS |
| Error | 614 | 107.71 | | |

Since sex and handedness have no great effect on modality raw scores or percentages, it is appropriate to collapse across these variables and examine the relationship between grade and modality scores. This could be accomplished by an analysis of variance, but a more descriptive approach is regression. The linear regression coefficient generated by a regression analysis is a readily understandable index of the relative rate of change of the dependent variables involved in the analysis, while the intercept values are good estimates of the means of the dependent variables at the smallest value of the independent variable.

Supplemental Table 17   COEFFICIENTS FOR THE REGRESSION OF MODALITY RAW SCORES AND PERCENTAGES ON GRADE

| Variable | Intercept | Linear Regression Coefficient |
|---|---|---|
| Visual raw score | 6.37 | 3.31 |
| Auditory raw score | 9.16 | 1.97 |
| Kinesthetic raw score | 3.78 | 3.23 |
| Visual percentage | 34.89 | .43 |
| Auditory percentage | 40.23 | − 1.64 |
| Kinesthetic percentage | 26.22 | .95 |

The intercept values reported in Supplemental Table 17 suggest that audition is the strongest modality, in terms of both raw scores and percentages, before a child enters school. Vision ranks second, while kinesthesia is the weakest. During the elementary school years, however, a substantial change occurs, and by the time a child is in sixth grade, vision has become the dominant modality, while audition is the least important.

The change that occurs between kindergarten and sixth grade can be explained by referring to the regression coefficients in Supplemental Table 17. These coefficients describe the rate of change of modality scores over time. In terms of modality raw scores, the coefficients for both vision and kinesthesia are greater than that of audition; all three coefficients are positive. This suggests that although all three scores are increasing during the elementary school years, audition is increasing at a slower rate than either vision or kinesthesia. With respect to percentage scores, the trend is even more noticeable. Vision and kinesthesia continue to increase, while the percentage scores for audition evidence a decrease, as reflected by a negative regression coefficient. In effect, audition is being supplanted as the dominant modality by both vision and kinesthesia. The lines of best fit corresponding to the analyses summarized in Supplemental Table 17 are shown in Supplemental Figures 1 and 2.

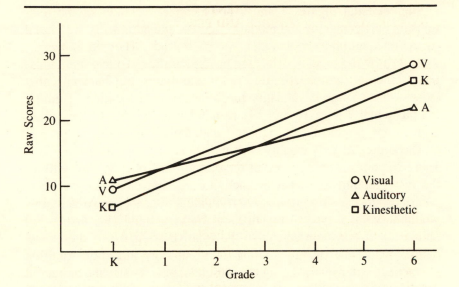

**Supplemental Figure 1   LINE OF BEST FIT FOR THE REGRESSION OF MODALITY RAW SCORES ON GRADE**

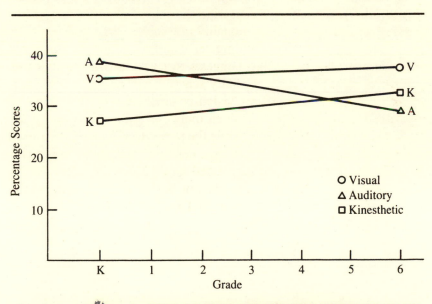

**Supplemental Figure 2   LINE OF BEST FIT FOR THE REGRESSION OF MODALITY PERCENTAGES ON GRADE**

Supplemental Figures 1 and 2 are idealized versions of the relationship between grade and modality scores, and admittedly are biased by the unequal number of students in each grade. They do, however, clearly show the modality shift we have identified. To avoid any misunderstanding, the reader is referred to the figures in Chapter IV that express the change in modality mean scores as a function of grade. Supplemental Tables 18 and 19 are tabular summaries of the values represented graphically in Figures 1 and 2 of Chapter IV.

The source of the modality shift indicated in Supplemental Figures 1 and 2 is not certain. We are of the opinion that reading and writing, the two predominant academic activities during elementary school, contribute to the shift. It appears reasonable that these two activities would serve as a type of practice for the visual and kinesthetic modalities, and that, consequently, the relative strengths of these modalities would increase in contrast to the auditory modality. Audition is practiced extensively during the preschool years, since the oral/aural mode is the principal means by which the young child interacts with adults and other children. It is, however, suppressed to a great extent in the classroom. The modality shift and the explanation we offer, then, appear reasonable, given the change in behavior that occurs between the preschool years and sixth grade.

**Supplemental Table 18   MODALITY RAW SCORES BROKEN DOWN BY GRADE**

| Grade | Number | Visual | | Auditory | | Kinesthetic | |
|-------|--------|--------|------|----------|------|-------------|-------|
|       |        | M      | SD   | M        | SD   | M           | SD    |
| K     | 81     | 9.74   | 6.91 | 11.39    | 6.53 | 8.04        | 5.98  |
| 1     | 100    | 12.69  | 6.57 | 12.33    | 5.23 | 10.22       | 5.32  |
| 2     | 118    | 15.64  | 8.01 | 15.86    | 5.47 | 13.00       | 9.90  |
| 3     | 85     | 21.97  | 8.98 | 17.18    | 6.18 | 17.28       | 8.99  |
| 4     | 99     | 22.87  | 9.52 | 19.31    | 6.05 | 20.91       | 10.58 |
| 5     | 92     | 26.91  | 8.80 | 20.10    | 7.68 | 22.33       | 11.22 |
| 6     | 62     | 27.52  | 10.80| 23.60    | 7.56 | 26.42       | 11.25 |
| Total | 637    | 19.18  | 10.50| 16.81    | 7.34 | 16.38       | 9.26  |

**Supplemental Table 19  MODALITY PERCENTAGES BROKEN DOWN BY GRADE**

| Grade | Number | Visual | | Auditory | | Kinesthetic | |
|---|---|---|---|---|---|---|---|
| | | M | SD | M | SD | M | SD |
| K | 81 | 32.74 | 12.77 | 39.68 | 12.48 | 27.58 | 12.90 |
| 1 | 100 | 35.73 | 14.02 | 35.14 | 11.19 | 29.13 | 11.79 |
| 2 | 118 | 34.87 | 11.11 | 37.35 | 10.80 | 27.78 | 9.58 |
| 3 | 85 | 38.73 | 10.05 | 31.23 | 8.81 | 30.04 | 9.87 |
| 4 | 99 | 36.09 | 8.31 | 31.95 | 8.28 | 31.95 | 8.92 |
| 5 | 92 | 39.71 | 10.35 | 29.27 | 7.61 | 31.02 | 9.76 |
| 6 | 62 | 35.30 | 8.90 | 31.36 | 8.88 | 33.34 | 8.94 |
| Total | 637 | 36.18 | 11.19 | 33.89 | 9.91 | 29.92 | 10.46 |

*Commentary.* The standardization research reported in Chapter IV and in this Appendix was conducted to justify the use of the Swassing-Barbe Modality Index as a classroom measurement tool. We are the first to admit, however, that our efforts were not so rigorous as we would wish. We conducted field-based research, and were unable to exercise as much administration and scoring control as would be possible in a laboratory setting. In addition to this shortcoming, there were several others:

1. The sample was not randomly selected.
2. The sample was not so large as that used to standardize some of the more popular achievement and intelligence tests. It was, however, as large or larger than most of the samples on which other modality instruments were based.
3. Our research was descriptive, not experimental. Causality can therefore only be assumed, and the validity of the instrument as a classification tool cannot be demonstrated.
4. The analysis of the data was not as thorough as it could have been. Many potentially relevant variables, such as socioeconomic status and parent modality strength, were ignored, and some of the interrelationships among the variables to which we did have access were not examined.
5. Variations in administration, scoring, and stimulus presentation were limited.

These shortcomings are not fatal, and characterize many psycho-educational instruments, particularly those used by teachers in a classroom setting. We would like to eliminate these shortcomings, however, and so are continuing to test the SBMI. Currently, we are engaged in a cross validation using a new sample; we are also studying the influence of teacher modality strengths on student achievement. Through ongoing research activities and the recommendations of teachers who use the SBMI, the instrument will be refined further.

## References

Dixon, W. J. (Ed.) *Biomedical computer programs: P-Series*. Berkeley: University of California, 1977.

McGraw-Hill. *Comprehensive Test of Basic Skills*. 1975.

Nie, N. H., Hull, C. H., Jenkins, J. G., Steinbrenner, K., and Bent, D. H. *Statistical package for the social sciences*. New York: McGraw-Hill, 1975.

# Selected Readings

Ackerman, P. R. *An evaluation of taxonomic teaching as a method for improving reading skills of emotionally disturbed, socially maladjusted boys*. Columbia University, New York, Research and Demonstration Center for the Education of Handicapped Children, 1971.

Anderson, R. G. A note on a case of spelling difficulty. *Journal of Applied Psychology*, 1938, *22*, 211–214.

Anderson, R. P. Physiologic considerations in learning: the tactile mode. In J. Helmuth (Ed.), *Learning Disorders* (Vol. III). Seattle: Special Child Publications, 1968.

Association for Supervision and Curriculum Development. Learning styles. *Educational Leadership*, 1979, *36*.

Atwood, B. S. Helping students recognize their own learning styles. *Learning*, 1975, *8*, 72–78.

Ausburn, F. B. *A comparison of multiple and linear image presentations of a comparative visual location task with visual and haptic college students*. Paper presented at the Association for Educational Communications and Technology Annual Convention, Dallas, Texas, 1975.

Ayres, A. J. *Southern California Motor Accuracy Test*. Los Angeles: Western Psychological Services, 1964.

―――. *Southern California Kinesthesia and Tactile Perception Tests*. Los Angeles: Western Psychological Services, 1966.

Balmuth, M. Visual and auditory modalities: How important are they? In N. B. Smith (Ed.), *Current Issues in Reading*. Newark, Del.: International Reading Association, 1969, 165–177.

Balow, B. Perceptual-motor activities in the treatment of severe reading disability. *The Reading Teacher*, 1971, *24*, 513–525.

Barbe, W. B. and Lucas, V. H. *Barbe-Lucas Handwriting Skill-Guide Check List*. Columbus, Ohio: Zaner-Bloser, 1978.

Bateman, B. The efficacy of an auditory and a visual method of first grade reading instruction with auditory and visual learners. In H. K. Smith (Ed.), *Perception and reading*. Newark, Del.: International Reading Association, 1968, 105–112.

Berman, A. The influence of the kinesthetic factors in the perception of symbols in partial reading disability. *Journal of Educational Psychology*, 1939, *30*, 187–198.

Blanton, B. Modalities and reading. *The Reading Teacher,* 1971, *25,* 210–212.

Bliesmer, E. P. and Yarborough, B. H. A comparison of ten different beginning reading programs in first grade. *Phi Delta Kappan,* 1965, *46,* 500–503.

Bloom, B. S. (Ed.) *Taxonomy of educational objectives. Handbook I: Cognitive domain.* New York: McKay, 1956.

Bracht, G. H. Experimental factors related to aptitude-treatment interactions. *Review of Educational Research,* 1970, *40,* 627–646.

Bruinicks, R. Relationship of auditory and visual perceptual strengths to methods of teaching word recognition among disadvantaged Negro boys. *Dissertation Abstracts,* 1969, *30A,* 1010-A.

————. Teaching word recognition to disadvantaged boys. *Journal of Learning Disabilities,* 1970, *3,* 28–36.

Bursuk, L. *Evaluation of correlated listening-reading comprehension lessons.* Paper presented at the meeting of the International Reading Association, 1971. (a)

————. *Sensory mode and lesson presentation as a factor in the reading comprehension improvement of adolescent retarded readers.* Doctoral dissertation, City University of New York, 1971. (b)

Camp, B. W. Learning rate and retention in retarded readers. *Journal of Learning Disabilities,* 1973, *6,* 65–71. (a)

————. Psychometric tests and learning in severely disabled readers. *Journal of Learning Disabilities,* 1973, *6,* 512–517. (b)

Chalfant, J. C. and Scheffelin, M. A. *Central processing dysfunctions in children: a review of research.* U.S. Department of Health, Education, and Welfare, National Institute of Neurological Diseases and Stroke, 1969.

Chall, J. S. *Learning to read: the great debate.* New York: McGraw-Hill, 1967.

Cooper, J. D. A study of learning modalities of good and poor first grade readers. In *Reading methods and teacher improvement.* Newark, Del.: International Reading Association, 1971.

Cronbach, L. J. and Snow, R. E. *Final report: Individual differences in learning ability as a function of instructional variables.* Stanford University, 1965. (ERIC Document Reproduction Service No. ED 029 001)

Cullinan, B., Ringler, E., and Smith, I. L. *Preferred learning modality and differential presentation of reading tasks.* Washington, D.C.: National Center for Educational Research and Development, 1969. (ERIC Document Reproduction Service No. ED 042 589)

Dechant, E. V. and Smith, H. P. *Psychology in teaching reading* (2nd ed.). Englewood Cliffs, NJ: Prentice-Hall, 1977.

DeHirsch, K., Jansky, J. J., and Langford, W. S. *Predicting reading failure.* New York: Harper and Row, 1966.

Dunn, R. and Dunn, K. *Learning Style Inventory*. Lawrence, Kan.: Price Systems, 1975.

————. How to diagnose learning styles. *Instructor,* 1977, *87,* 122–144. (a)

————. Seeing, hearing, moving, touching learning packages. *Teacher,* 1977, *94,* 48–51. (b)

————. Learning styles/teaching styles: should they . . . can they . . . be matched? *Educational Leadership,* 1979, *36,* 238–244.

————. *Teaching students through their individual learning styles*. Reston, Virginia: Reston Publishing Company, 1978.

Epstein, W. *Varieties of perceptual learning*. New York: McGraw-Hill, 1967.

Estes, R. E. and Stewart, J. C. *A comparison of visual and auditory channels in learning disabled and control children*. Paper presented at the Annual Meeting of the American Educational Research Association, Washington, D.C., 1975.

Fernald, G. M. A study of reading disability in adults. *Psychological Bulletin,* 1933, *30,* 595.

————. *Remedial techniques in basic school subjects*. New York: McGraw-Hill, 1943.

Fernald, G. M. and Keller, H. The effect of kinesthetic factors in the development of word recognition in the case of non-readers. *Journal of Educational Research,* 1921, *4,* 355–377.

————. On certain language disabilities. *Mental Measurements Monograph,* Number 11. Baltimore: Williams and Wilkins, 1936.

Forster, M. Visual and visual-kinesthetic learning in reading nonsense syllables. *Journal of Educational Psychology,* 1941, *32,* 452–458.

Foster, G. G., Reese, J. H., Schmidt, C. R., and Ohrtman, W. F. Modality preference and the learning of sight words. *Journal of Special Education,* 1976, *10,* 253–258.

Freer, F. *Visual and auditory perceptual modality differences as related to success in first grade word recognition*. Unpublished doctoral dissertation, Rutgers University, 1971.

French, E. L. Kinesthetic recognition in retarded readers. *Educational and Psychological Measurement,* 1953, *13,* 637.

Friedland, S. J. and Shilkret, R. B. Alternative explanations of learning disabilities: defensive hyperactivity. *Exceptional Children,* 1973, *40,* 213–215.

Frostig, M. and Horne, D. *The Frostig program for the development of visual perception*. Chicago: Follett, 1964.

Frostig, M., Maslow, P., and Lefever, W. *The Marianne Frostig Developmental Test of Visual Perception*. Palo Alto, Calif.: Consulting Psychologists Press, 1963.

Fry, E. Comparison of beginning reading with i.t.a., DMS, and t.o. after three years. *The Reading Teacher,* 1969, *22,* 357–362.

Geissal, M. A. and Knafle, J. A linguistic view of auditory discrimination tests and exercises. *The Reading Teacher,* 1977, *30,* 134–141.

Gentry, L. A. A clinical method in classroom success—kinesthetic teaching. *The Reading Teacher,* 1974, *28,* 298–300.

Gibson, E. J. and Levin, H. *The psychology of reading.* Cambridge, Mass.: Massachusetts Institute of Technology Press, 1975.

Gillespie, P. H. and Johnson, L. *Teaching reading to the mildly retarded child.* Columbus, Ohio: Charles E. Merrill, 1974.

Gould, L. N. *An optometrist looks at perceptions.* Paper presented at the International Reading Association Conference, Kansas City, Mo., 1969.

Gurren, L. and Hughes, A. Intensive phonics vs. gradual phonics in beginning reading: a review. *The Journal of Educational Research,* 1965, *58,* 339–346.

Hallahan, D. P. Distractibility in the learning disabled child. In W. M. Cruickshank and D. P. Hallahan (Eds.), *Perceptual and learning disabilities in children* (Vol. 2). Syracuse: Syracuse University Press, 1975.

Hallahan, D. P. and Cruickshank, W. M. *Psychoeducational foundations of learning disabilities.* Englewood Cliffs, NJ: Prentice-Hall, 1973.

Harris, A. J. *Individualizing first grade reading according to specific learning aptitudes.* New York: City University of New York, 1965.

Harris, A. J. and Sipay, E. R. *How to increase reading ability* (6th ed.). New York: David McKay, 1975.

Henmon, V. A. C. The relationship between mode of presentation and retention. *Psychological Review,* 1912, *19,* 79–96.

Humphrey, J. J. and Sullivan, D. D. *Teaching reading through motor learning.* Springfield, Ill.: Charles C. Thomas, 1973.

Itard, J. M. G. *The wild boy of Aveyron.* (G. Humphrey and M. Humphrey trans.) New York: The Century Company, 1932.

Janssen, D. R. *Effects of visual and auditory perceptual aptitudes and letter discrimination pretraining on word recognition.* Unpublished doctoral dissertation, Pennsylvania State University, 1972.

Johnson, D. J. and Myklebust, H. R. *Learning disabilities: educational principles and practices.* New York: Grune and Stratton, 1967.

Jones, J.P. *Intersensory transfer, perceptual shifting, modal preference, and reading.* Newark, Del.: International Reading Association, 1971.

Kalin, M. F. and McAvoy, R. *The influence of choice on the acquisition and retention of learning materials in different modes of instruction.* Paper presented at the Annual Meeting of the American Educational Research Association, New Orleans, 1975.

Kanner, L. Itard, Seguin, Howe—three pioneers in the education of retarded children. *American Journal of Mental Deficiency,* 1961, *66,* 2.

Kephart, N. C. *The slow learner in the classroom.* Columbus, Ohio: Merrill, 1960.

Kirk, S. A. The influence of manual training on the learning of simple words in the case of subnormal boys. *Journal of Educational Psychology,* 1933, *24,* 525–535.

Kirk, S. A. and Kirk, W. D. *Psycholinguistic learning disabilities: diagnosis and remediation.* Urbana: University of Illinois, 1971.

Kirk, S. A., McCarthy, J. J., and Kirk, W. D. *Illinois Test of Psycholinguistic Abilities* (Experimental Ed.). Urbana: University of Illinois, 1961.

———. *Illinois Test of Psycholinguistic Abilities.* Urbana: University of Illinois: 1968.

Klatzky, R. L. *Human memory: structure and processes.* San Francisco: Freeman, 1975.

Kramer, R. *Maria Montessori.* New York: Putnam, 1976.

Lane, H. *The wild boy of Aveyron.* Cambridge, Mass.: Harvard University, 1976.

Lee, G. and Young, V. Auditory vs. visual: a dual modality theory. *The Record,* 1974, *11,* 28–30.

Lilly, M. S. and Kelleher, J. Modality strengths and aptitude-treatment interaction. *Journal of Special Education,* 1973, *7,* 5–13.

Lumpkin, D. *Assessing "word learning" modes and word recognition.* Paper presented at the meeting of the International Reading Association, Atlantic City, NJ, 1971.

Maccoby, E. E. and Jacklin, C. N. *The psychology of sex differences.* Palo Alto, Calif.: Stanford University Press, 1974.

McCarthy, W. and Oliver, J. Some tactile-kinesthetic procedures for teaching reading to slow learning children. *Exceptional Children,* 1965, *31,* 419–421.

Mann, L. et al. *Sensory modality preferences: measurement of selected psychological "process" variables and their validity: implications of aptitude-treatment interaction research with learning disabled children.* Montgomery County Intermediate Unit 23, Blue Bell, Pennsylvania, 1975.

McCracken, R. A. A comparative study of modalities in beginning reading instruction. *The Reading Teacher,* 1974, *28,* 6–9.

Meehan, T. An informal modality inventory. *Elementary English,* 1974, *51,* 901–904.

Mills, R. E. *The teaching of word recognition.* Ft. Lauderdale: The Mills School, 1970.

Montessori, M. *The Montessori method*. New York: Stokes, 1912.

———. *Dr. Montessori's own handbook*. New York: Schochen, 1914.

Morency, A. Auditory modality, research and practices. In H. K. Smith (Ed.), *Perception and reading*. Newark, Del.: International Reading Association, 1968, 17–21.

Mozingo, L. L. *An investigation of auditory and visual modality preferences for teaching word recognition skills to students classified as auditory or visual learners*. Doctoral dissertation, University of South Carolina, 1978.

Myers, C. A. Reviewing the literature on Fernald's technique of remedial reading. *The Reading Teacher*, 1978, *31*, 614–619.

Myers, G. C. *The learner and his attitude*. New York: Sanborn, 1925.

Newcomer, P. L. *Construct validity of the Illinois Test of Psycholinguistic Abilities*. Unpublished doctoral dissertation, Temple University, 1973.

Newcomer, P. L. and Goodman, L. Effect of modality of instruction on the learning of meaningful and nonmeaningful material by auditory and visual learners. *Journal of Special Education*, 1975, *9*, 261–268.

O'Brien, D. E. *A functional analysis of the learning modalities of gifted children*. Unpublished master's thesis, The Ohio State University, 1978.

Orton, S. T. *Reading, writing, and speech problems in children*. New York: Norton, 1937.

Pearson, C. Do you know how to Chisanbop? *Learning*, 1978, *7*, 134–138.

Potts, M. The relative achievement of first graders under three different reading programs. *The Journal of Educational Research*, 1968, *61*, 447–450.

Reissman, F. Students' learning styles: how to determine, strengthen, and capitalize on them. *Today's Education*, 1976, *65*, 94–98.

Reynolds, M. C. A study of the relationship between auditory characteristics and specific silent reading abilities. *Journal of Educational Psychology*, 1941, *32*, 452–458.

Ringler, L. H. and Smith, I. L. Learning modality and word recognition of first grade children. *Journal of Learning Disabilities*, 1973, *6*, 38–43.

Robinson, H. M. Visual and auditory modalities related to method of beginning reading instruction. *Reading Research Quarterly*, 1972, *8*, 7–39.

Sabatino, D. A., Abbott, J. C., and Becker, J. T. What does the Frostig DTVP measure? *Exceptional Children*, 1974, *40*, 453–454.

Sabatino, D. A. and Dorfman, N. Matching learner aptitude to two commercial reading programs. *Exceptional Children*, 1974, *40*, 85–90.

Sabatino, D. A. and Hayden, D. L. Prescriptive teaching in a summer learning disabilities program. *Journal of Learning Disabilities*, 1970, *3*, 220–227.

Sabatino, D. A. and Streissguth, W. D. Word form configuration training of visual perceptual strengths with learning disabled children. *Journal of Learning Disabilities*, 1972, *5*, 435–441.

Sabatino, D. A., Ysseldyke, J. E., and Woolston, J. Diagnostic-prescriptive perceptual training with mentally retarded children. *American Journal of Mental Deficiency,* 1973, *78,* 7–14.

Silberberg, N. E., Iverson, I. A., and Goins, J. T. Which remedial method works best? *Journal of Learning Disabilities,* 1973, *6,* 547–556.

Slingerland, B. H. *Specific language disability children, a multisensory approach to language arts: a guide for primary teachers.* Cambridge, Mass.: Educator's Publishing Service, 1975.

Smith, C. M. The relationship of reading method and reading achievement to ITPA sensory modalities. *Journal of Special Education,* 1971, *5,* 143–149.

Smith, I. L. and Ringler, L. H. Preferred sensory modality, reading readiness, and reading achievement in first grade children. *Perceptual and Motor Skills,* 1971, *32,* 764–766.

Standing, E. M. *Maria Montessori: her life and work.* New York: Mentor-Omega, 1962.

Stober, M. and Fields, W. *Modality linking: selection of activities and materials.* City University of New York, Center for Advanced Study in Education, 1974.

Strauss, A. A. and Kephart, N. C. *Psychopathology and education of the brain-injured child: Volume II. Progress in theory and clinic.* New York: Grune and Stratton, 1955.

Strauss, A. A. and Lehtinen, L. E. *Psychopathology and education of the brain-injured child.* New York: Grune and Stratton, 1947.

Stuart, I. R. Perceptual style and reading ability: implications for an instructional approach. *Perceptual and Motor Skills,* 1967, *24,* 135–138.

Swassing, R. H. Parameters of classroom environment for the beginning teacher. *Education and Training of the Mentally Retarded,* 1974, *9,* 89–92.

Tarver, S. G. and Dawson, M. M. Modality preference and the teaching of reading: a review. *Journal of Learning Disabilities,* 1978, *11,* 17–29.

Terman, L. M. Foreword. In G. M. Fernald, *Remedial techniques in basic school subjects.* New York: McGraw-Hill, 1943.

Vandever, T. R. and Neville, D. D. Modality aptitude and word recognition. *Journal of Reading Behavior,* 1974, *2,* 195–201.

Vernon, M. D. Visual perception relating to reading-information sources. *The Reading Teacher,* 1974, *28,* 184–186.

Wallace, G. and Kauffman, J. M. *Teaching children with learning problems.* Columbus, Ohio: Charles E. Merrill, 1973.

Waugh, R. *Modality preference as a function of reading achievement.* Eugene, Oregon: Oregon University, Dept. of Special Education, 1971.

————. Comparison of revised and experimental editions of the ITPA. *Journal of Learning Disabilities*, 1973, *6*, 236–238. (a)

————. Relationship between modality preference and performance. *Exceptional Children*, 1973, *39*, 465–469. (b)

————. The ITPA: ballast or bonanza for the school psychologist? *Journal of School Psychology*, 1975, *13*, 201–208.

Waugh, R. and Watson, L. Visual perception and reading. *Education*, 1970, *91*, 181–183.

Wepman, J. M. *Auditory Discrimination Test*. Chicago: Language Research Associates, 1958.

————. Modalities and learning. In H. M. Robinson (Ed.), *Coordinating reading instruction*. Glenview, Ill.: Scott Foresman, 1971.

————. The modality concept: including a statement of the perceptual and conceptual levels of learning. In H. K. Smith (Ed.), *Perception and Reading*. Newark, Del.: International Reading Association, 1968, 1–6.

————. The perceptual basis for learning. In E. C. Frierson and W. B. Barbe (Eds.), *Educating children with learning disabilities*. New York: Appleton-Century-Crofts, 1967.

Williams, D. U. and Williams, J. P. *Children's verbal learning and comprehension in the aural and visual modes*. Paper presented at the meeting of the American Educational Research Association, Chicago, Ill., 1972.

Wolpert, E. M. Modality and reading: a perspective. *The Reading Teacher*, 1971, *24*, 640–643.

Yamamoto, K. Stimulus mode and sensory modality: What's in it for education? *The Record*, 1969, *70*, 513–521.

Ysseldyke, J. E. Diagnostic-prescriptive teaching: the search for aptitude-treatment interactions. In L. Mann and D. Sabatino (Eds.), *The first review of special education*. Philadelphia: Journal of Special Education Press, 1973.

Zeaman, D. and House, B. J. The role of attention in retardate discrimination learning. In N. R. Ellis (Ed.), *Handbook of mental deficiency: psychological theory and practice*. New York: McGraw-Hill, 1963.

# Index of Names

Barbe, W.B., 28, 31, 34, 46, 47, 66
Barbe, W.B. and Lucas, V.H., 66
Binet, A., 33
Bloom, B.S., 56
Chalfant, J.C., 52
Chalfant, J.C. and Scheffelin, M.A., 52
Condillac, E.B. de, 20, 29, 32, 73
Dawson, M.M., 11, 12, 13
Dechant, E.V., 34
Dechant, E.V. and Smith, H.P., 34
Dixon, W.J., 85
Dunn, R. and Dunn, K., 13, 28, 34
Epstein, W., 1
Fernald, G.M., 18, 24, 25, 29, 73
Froebel, F., 20
Frostig, M., 28, 29, 73
Frostig, M. and Horne, D., 28
Fry, E., 13
Horne, D., 28
Itard, J.M.G., 20, 21, 22, 25, 29, 32, 73
Jacklin, C.N., 51
Kephart, N.C., 26, 27, 29, 73
Kirk, S.A., 27, 28, 29, 33, 73
Kirk, S.A., McCarthy, J.J., and Kirk, W., 27, 33, 88
Klatsky, R., 2
Kramer, R., 20, 22, 23, 24
Lane, H., 20, 21, 22
Lehtinen, L.E., 26, 29, 73
Lucas, V.H., 66
Maccoby, H.S., 51

Maccoby, H.S. and Jacklin, C.N., 51
Massieu, J., 21
Mills, R.E., 12, 13, 28, 29, 33
Montessori, M., 15, 22, 23, 24, 25, 26, 27, 29, 32, 73
Mozingo, L.L., 13
Myers, G.C., 16
Nie, N.H., et al., 85
Orton, S.T., 25, 26, 73
Pavlov, I., 22
Pearson, C., 67
Pereira, J., 20, 22
Pestalozzi, J.H., 20
Pinel, P., 20
Rousseau, J.J., 19, 20, 29, 32, 73
Scheffelin, M.A., 52
Seguin, E., 22, 32, 73
Sicard, Abbe de, 21
Simon, T., 33
Smith, H.P., 34
Strauss, A.A., 26, 27, 29, 73
Strauss, A.A. and Kephart, N.C., 26, 27, 29
Strauss, A.A. and Lehtinen, L.E., 26, 29
Swassing, R.H., 28, 31, 34, 46, 47
Swassing, R.H. and Barbe, W.B., 28, 31, 34, 46, 47
Tarver, S.G., 11, 12, 13
Tarver, S.G. and Dawson, M.M., 11, 12, 13
Victor, (Wild Boy of Aveyron), 20, 21, 22, 32
Wepman, J.M., 3
Witty, P.A., vii

# Index of Subjects

Abacus, 67
Achievement, as related to SBMI, 50
Age, and grade placement, 51–53
Age of Enlightenment, 19
Analysis of variance, 91–95
Arithmetic
  kinesthetic teaching methods, 67
  modality-based instruction in, 67–68
  visual teaching method, 68
Audition, decrease in importance of, through elementary school years, 52
Auditory and speech training, 22
Auditory classroom, 8
Auditory learner, 58
  characteristics of, 44–45
  as slow reader, 66
Auditory teacher, 14, 15
Auto-educational materials, 22–23
Auto race analogy, 12

Basic skills, importance of modality-based instruction to, 64
Behavior
  covert, 2
  human, 3
  indicative of modality strength, 44–45
  overt, 2
  sensation and, 5
Biomedical Computer Program, P-Series, 85
Brain-injured children, 26
Brain regions, 3

Cafeteria approach, appeal of, 57
  limitations of, 57
Chisanbop, 67
Civilization, increasing demands placed on individual, 27
Clinic School, U.C.L.A., 24
Coefficient of reproducibility, 50, 87
Coefficient of scalability, 51, 87
Cognitive development, and modality strength, 52
Cognitive strategies, 6
Compositor's table, 21
Comprehensive Tests of Basic Skills, 50, 88
Configuration cues, for spelling, 59–60
Construct validity (see Validity, construct)
Continuity, importance of, in self-instruction, 63
Correlation matrix, 89–91
Correlational analysis, 88
Cuisinaire rods, 67
Curriculum modifications, 13
Curriculum recommendations, 6

Deaf children, 20, 22
Deficit-oriented approach, 56
Discrimination training, 21
Dominant modality
  definition of, 6, 71
  as determined by SBMI, 40
  observation of, 6, 44–45
  reliance upon, in early elementary grades, 64
  reversion to, under stress, 6

Educational change, impetus, 19
Educational testing, goal of, 31
*Enfant sauvage,* 21

Fernald's approach
  application of, 25
  key elements of, 24–25
  stages in, 24
F-ratio, 92–95
Frostig's program
  assessment tool, 28
  elements of, 28
  limitations of, 28

Games, instructional, 66
Geometric shapes, matching, 21
Grade placement, 52
Grade placement, and age, 51–53, 95–99
Grouping, 58, 70
Grouping, by modality, 62, 63
  critical features of, 63
  efficiency of, 63

Handedness
  establishing, 36
  and scores on SBMI, 51, 94–95
Handwriting
  auditory teaching method, 67
  instruction, modality-based, 66–67
  kinesthetic nature of, 66
  kinesthetic teaching method, 67
  visual teaching method, 66
Hemispheric dominance, 52
History of modality-based instruction, commentary on, 28–30
Homonyms, spelling, for kinesthetic learners, 70
Human development, and learning, 3

Illinois Test of Psycholinguistic Abilities (ITPA), 27, 28, 29, 33, 46, 88

limitations of, 33
Imagination, and modality, 16
Individualized instruction, 20, 58
Information, transmission of, 18
Initial instruction, 58–60, 72
  adaptation of, 61
  failure of, 55
  modification to, 55
Initial objectives, selection of, 56
Initial teaching strategies (*see* Initial instruction)
Institute for Deaf-Mutes, 20–21
Instruction
  adaptation of, into teacher's strongest modality, 58
  of mentally retarded, 22
  using multisensory materials, 16
Integration of modalities (*see also* Modalities, integration of)
  advantage of, 58
Intelligence, as fixed characteristic, 33
Intelligence tests
  as indices of learning strengths, 31
  lack of value for educators, 33
  negative effects of, 31
  relationship with modality strengths, 33
Intelligence quotient, interpretation of, 31
Interference, among modalities, 16, 42, 70
Intercept values, 96
Interindividual differences, 27
Intraindividual differences, 27
Itard's method, shortcoming of, 22
ITPA (see Illinois Test of Psycholinguistic Abilities)

Kindergarten, 20
Kinesthesia (*see* Kinesthetic modality)

Kinesthetic classroom, 9
Kinesthetic learner
  characteristics of, 44–45, 60
  example of, 60
Kinesthetic learning
  direct, 65
  games for, 66
  vicarious activity in, 65
Kinesthetic methods, of Montes-
    sori, 23
Kinesthetic modality
  definition of, 5
  components of, 5, 71
  as a composite ability, 5–6
Kinesthetic perception, binding vi-
    sion and audition, 26
Kinesthetic teacher, 15
  classroom organization of, 15
  relationship with peers and su-
    pervisors, 15
Kinesthetic teaching, history of,
    18
Kirk's approach, components of,
    27
Knowledge, and application, 56

Labeling, 43, 58
Large-muscle activities, in spell-
    ing, 69
Learning
  comparison of three children,
    with different modality
    strengths, 58–62
  components, 27
  conditions under which it oc-
    curs best, 4
  effects of reinforcement and
    motivation on, 4
  efficiency of, 7
  exemplary, 4
  human development and, 3
  keys to, 1
  outcomes, 63
  process of, according to
    Strauss, 27

Learning Methods Test, 12, 28,
    29, 33, 34
  limitations of, 34
Learning strengths, 23
Learning styles
  adaptation of, 64
  teaching styles and, 13
Learning Style Inventory, 28, 34
  limitation of, 34
Letter recognition, 21
Linear regression coefficient, 96

Memorization
  importance of, in arithmetic, 67
  in Greek teaching, 18
  preference for, 19, 29
Memory
  components of, 2
  definition of, 2
  long term, 2, 3
  short term, 2, 3, 50
  storehouse, 2
  superiority associated with audi-
    tory and visual, 29
  workshop analogy, 2
Mixed modality
  classroom advantage of, 6
  comparative proportions of,
    among adults and children, 6
  definition of, 6, 71
  as function of cognitive devel-
    opment, 6
Modalities
  changes in relative strength of,
    52–53, 85–100
  as channels, 1, 5
  delay of integration of, 58
  educationally relevant, 5, 71
  as essential to everyday func-
    tioning, 25
  integration of, 6, 16, 26, 52, 64
  integration of, with age, 27
  interference among, 16, 42, 70
  transferring cues among, 59, 61

Modality
  capitalizing on stronger, 26
  concepts, 1–17, 71
  constituent elements of, 1
  definition of, 1–3, 71
  environmental influence on, 3
  as a fixed neurologic character-
    istic, 3, 71–72
  interaction between dominant
    and secondary, 6
  limitation of fixed characteristic
    perspective, 3
  as measurable behavior, 5
  neurological basis of, 3
  three aspects of, 15, 71
  three views of, 3–5
Modality-based education (*see*
  Modality-based instruction)
Modality-based instruction, 5, 7,
  28, 55–70, 72–73
  antecedents of, 18
  applications of, 70
  in arithmetic, 67–68
  in basic skill areas, 64, 70
  for brain-injured children, 26
  in content areas, 70
  contrasted with conventional
    methods, 12
  contrasted with multisensory in-
    struction, 57
  as currently practiced by teach-
    ers, 8
  definition of, 55
  effectiveness of, 75
  efficiency of, 75
  examples of classrooms in
    which teachers have different
    strengths, 8–11
  failure of, 11
  as framework for teaching, 70
  fundamentals of, 13–16
  grade levels, applied at, 56
  grouping for, 58
  in handwriting, 66
  history of, 18–30, 73

  illustrations of, 58–62
  increased rate of learning with,
    7
  indirect support for, 12
  initial teaching strategies in,
    55–70
  Kirk's method of, 27
  lack of curriculum for, 29
  lack of support for, by educa-
    tors, 18, 28–30
  learning disabilities and, 27
  logical basis of, 7–8
  practice of, 55–70
  promise of, 73–75
  in reading, 65–66
  reasons for its failure to become
    popular, 29
  as remediation, 27, 29, 62
  research concerning, 11–13
  research support of, 12
  in spelling, 68–69
  strength orientation of, 56,73
  substantiation of, 13
  Tarver and Dawson's criticism
    of, 11–13
  two forms of, 70
  two stages involved in, 8
  what it is, 55
  what it is not, 56–58
Modality-based reinforcement,
  61–62
Modality-based teaching (*see*
  Modality-based instruction)
Modality, dominant (*see* Dominant modality)
Modality, mixed (*see* Mixed
  modality)
Modality preference, 4, 34
  limitations of, 4
  reliability of, 4
  social acceptability, 4
  validity of, 4
Modality, secondary (*see*
  Secondary modality)

Modality shift, explanation
  of, 11, 96–99
Modality strength, 71
  adaptation of, 58, 64
  assessment, 29, 32, 33, 34, 71–72
  assessment by observation, 32
  assessment, limitations of
    previous, 29, 46
  awareness of, 14, 15, 26, 55,
    58, 72
  changes in, 11, 52–53
  conflict between teacher's and
    student's, 62
  and cognitive development, 52
  in contrast to modality prefer-
    ence, 5, 72
  differences of, among neonates, 4
  dominant (*see* Dominant
    modality)
  efficiency of sensory pathways, 3
  examples of, 41–43
  hereditary factors in, 3
  heredity and environment, role
    of, in shaping, 5
  identification of, 31–46
  illustration of children with
    different strengths, 7
  as influenced by education, 52
  interaction between student's,
    and teaching methods, 11
  match between student and
    teacher, 64
  mixed (*see* Mixed modality)
  observable characteristics
    of, 43–45
  as physiologic characteristic, 3
  as a predisposition, 4
  previous efforts at assess-
    ment, 32–35
  problems of identification in
    previous research, 11
  projection of one's own, 44
  as reflected in teaching
    styles, 8–10
  relationship with intelligence
    tests, 33

  relative importance of, 52
  secondary (*see* Secondary
    modality)
  selection of materials for, 58
  of teacher, 14, 36, 58
  of teacher, influence on
    instruction, 64
  of teachers and students, 55
  teaching to (*see* Modality-
    based instruction)
  tests of (*see* Modality strengths,
    assessment)
  three profiles, 41–43
  variations in individuals, 26
Montessori approach
  sequence of activities in, 23
  reasons for failure of, 24
Montessori-type methods, 15
Motor coordination, 22
Multisensory education, 28
Multisensory instruction, 57
  contrasted with modality-
    based instruction, 57
  drawbacks of, 57
Multisensory materials, 57
Multisensory stimulation, in
  Fernald's method, 24–25

Natural education, 19
Neonates, differences in
  modality strengths of, 4

Objectives, importance of, in
  self-instruction, 63
Orton's technique, reasons
  for lack of recognition, 25

Perception, 1, 3
  definition of, 1
Personalized instruction, 13,
  22, 26, 58
Phonics, 56
  with auditory learners, 13
  failure of, for non-auditory
    teachers, 14

with visual learners, 56
Physiology, 22
Play, as stimulation to
    learning, 20
Point of intervention, 13, 55,
    62, 70, 72
    in remedial situations, 62
    two approaches, 62–64
Proactive inhibition, 57
Psychological tests, 24, 29

Reading
    auditory teaching method, 66
    as covert behavior, 2
    history of teaching, 18
    instruction, initial goals
        in, 65
    instruction, phonetic approach
        to, 56
    kinesthetic approaches to,
        65–66
    subvocalization in, 66
    use of finger pointing in, 65
    as visual process, 65
Regression analysis, 95–99
Reinforcement, modality-based,
    61–62
Reliability, 48, 50, 87
    coefficient of reproducibility,
        50, 87
    coefficient of scalability,
        51, 87
    example of, 48
    Guttman scale, 50, 87
    internal consistency, 50
    stability, 50, 88
    test-retest, 88
Reproducibility, coefficient of,
    50, 87
Retroactive inhibition, 57
Rose analogy, 16

SBMI (*see* Swassing-Barbe
    Modality Index)
Scalability, coefficient of, 51, 87
Scheffe test, 92

Secondary modality
    as determined by SBMI, 41
    definition, 6, 71
    efficiency of, 6
Self-instructional materials,
    62, 63, 64, 70
    conditions for, 63
Sensation, 1, 3, 71–72
    and behavior, 2, 5
    definition of, 1
Sensationalism, 20
Sense experience, key to
    learning, 20
Sensory channels, 1
Sensory organ, 3
Sensory strength (*see* Modality
    strengths)
Sensory stimulation, as first
    step to learning, 23
Shotgun approach, limitations
    of, 57
Spelling
    auditory method of, 68
    errors, relationship with
        modality strengths, 69–70
    instruction, for kinesthetic
        learners, 63
    kinesthetic methods of, 69
    visual method of, 68
Stability (*see* Reliability)
Standardization research
    generalizability of findings, 48
    procedures 48, 85
Standardization sample,
    relationship of, to national
    percentages, 47, 85
Statistical package for the
    Social Sciences, 85
Strauss and Lehtinen's techniques,
    components of, 26
Swassing-Barbe Modality Index,
    28, 31–51 passim
    achievement and, 50
    administration of, 36–38, 39
    administration time for, 36
    auditory subtest in, 38

Swassing-Barbe Modality Index (cont'd.)
as a behavioral sample, 32
changes in scores over grade or age, 51–53, 96–99
coefficient of reproducibility, 50, 87
coefficient of scalability, 87
comparison of Hispanic and general students' perform- ances on, 47, 85
comparison of left and right- handed students' performance on, 51–53, 94–95
comparison of males' and fe- males' performance on, 51– 53, 92–93
completion of testing, 37, 38
computer programs used in standardization research, 85
consistency in administration of, 39
criterion validity of, 49
description of, 35–36, 42, 46, 72
development of, 34–35
early form of, 35
errors in middle of child's response, 39
establishing handedness, 36
establishing rapport, 36
extra shapes in response, 39
face or logical validity of, 49
handedness and, 51, 94–95
indirect validity of, 50, 87
internal consistency of, 50
interpretation of, 40
interruptions during adminis- tration of, 38
justification for, 34
kinesthetic subtest in, 38
as a matching-to-sample task, 35
observing the child during, 32, 41–43

percentage scores, computing, 40, 78–83
percentage scores, educationally relevant difference, 40
pre-administration, 36
psychometric properties of, 48–51, 85–90
regression analysis, 95–99
reliability of, 50, 87–88
repeating instructions, 37
reversals in response, 39
sample items, 35
scoring, 37–41
sex differences, 51, 92–93
specifications underlying development of, 35
stability of, 50, 87–88
standardization of, 47–53, 85– 100
standardization research, limitations of, 99–100
standardization sample, 47, 85
stimulus control, 36
stimulus forms, 35
strength orientation, 31–32
technical report of standard- ization, 85–100
testing surface, 36
timing recommendation, 37
use for skilled observer, 43
validity, 49, 87
validity and reliability, 46, 87
verbal direction in, 37–38
visual subtest of, 37

Tactile discrimination, 22
Taxonomy of Educational Objectives, 56
Teacher, as guide, 23
greatest concern of, 7
Teaching through modality strengths, 56–57 (see also Modality-based instruction)
Test-retest reliability (see Reliability)

Testing movement, emphasis of, 31

Things as teachers, 23

Tracing, 19, 24

Traditional instruction, constraints of, 23

Transfer of information among modalities, 59

University of California at Los Angeles Clinic School, 24

Validity, 48, 49, 85
    construct, 49, 85
    criterion, 49
    example of, 48

face or logical, 49, 85
factor analysis of, 49, 86
indirect, 50

Varimax rotation, 87

Vision, importance of, 25–26

Visual association, 25, 65

Visual classroom, 9–10

Visual learner
    characteristics of, 44–45
    example of, 59

Visual teacher, 15

Visual-auditory teaching, history of, 18

Word configuration, 15, 59

Word file, 25

Writing, history of teaching, 18